THE EDUCATION
OF THE
HEARING IMPAIRED

THE EDUCATION
OF THE
HEARING IMPAIRED

Second Printing

By

C. JOSEPH GIANGRECO, ED. D.

Superintendent, Iowa School for the Deaf
Council Bluffs, Iowa

and

MARIANNE RANSON GIANGRECO, M. S.

Instructor, Iowa School for the Deaf
Council Bluffs, Iowa

With a Foreword by
Marshall S. Hiskey, Ph. D.

Coordinator of Special Education
and
Director, Educational-Psychological Clinic
University of Nebraska
Lincoln, Nebraska

CHARLES C THOMAS · PUBLISHER
Springfield · *Illinois* · *U.S.A.*

Published and Distributed Throughout the World by

CHARLES C THOMAS ● PUBLISHER

Bannerstone House

301-327 East Lawrence Avenue, Springfield, Illinois, U.S.A.

© *1970, by* CHARLES C THOMAS ● PUBLISHER

ISBN 0-398-00673-3

Library of Congress Catalog Card Number: 78-83834

First Printing, 1970
Second Printing, 1976

With THOMAS BOOKS *careful attention is given to all details of
manufacturing and design. It is the Publisher's desire to present books that are
satisfactory as to their physical qualities and artistic possibilities and
appropriate for their particular use.* THOMAS BOOKS *will be true to those
laws of quality that assure a good name and good will.*

Printed in the United States of America

R-1

To Carmella and Michael Giangreco—
Parents with a vision,

And Evanda and Gail Ranson—
Parents with energy and awareness of opportunity,

And to all children with impaired hearing—
The book's inspiration.

FOREWORD

THIS IS A BOOK about the personal, social and, especially, educational problems related to children and youth who have serious deficiencies of hearing. The authors share with the reader the results of twenty years of close personal association with deaf children, their teachers and their parents.

In general, the points of view which are reflected are those of the authors with little attempt to lean heavily on theory or upon what might be classified as standardized practices. There is a sincere attempt to promote an understanding and appreciation of the deaf and to provide suggestions for teachers, parents, and professionals which are based on actual experiences and procedures. Whereas this volume is not intended as a text, it has much to offer the student in training. It has been stated that to produce a successful handicapped person requires that four ingredients be favorably mixed together: the handicapped person, the parents, the school and the community. The contents of this book include messages to each of the four.

As an introduction to present day situations, the authors have compiled a brief but excellent history of the Deaf as men have regarded them through the centuries. The Old Testament reveals that the Hebrews had special laws pertaining to the deaf as early as 500 B.C. It is recorded that one of the miracles of Jesus was the granting of speech and hearing to a deaf mute. Aristotle provided the most direct and far-reaching impact on the lives of those who endured the handicap of deafness. His well-meaning, but completely inaccurate and misdirected, evaluations and descriptions of the results of deafness sentenced the deaf to centuries of bondage, hopelessness, and despair. During the many centuries which followed, the deaf were considered fools or idiots, odd, depraved, listless, uneducable, doomed souls, and incapable of participating in civic affairs. Observers reported them to be treacherous, cruel, melancholy, suspicious, self-willed and dumb.

The educational successes with a few deaf persons in the 16th and 17th centuries were little less than miracles, but for the first time the parents of deaf children had a ray of hope. Many decades were to pass, however, before broad educational opportunities became a reality. During the past century much progress has been made, but the problems of providing more meaningful experiences for the deaf in the school and in the community continue to frustrate and to challenge us.

Although no hearing person can ever divorce himself from sound to the extent that he can understand what living in a silent world is really like, Dr. and Mrs. Joseph Giangreco's many years of association with the deaf make them ideally suited for the presentations which are made in this book.

The Giangreco's realize that the deaf child often develops in a family and world that have many misconceptions about his disabilities. If a child's hearing loss was present at birth and is severe, he goes through early life without the comfort and reassurance of listening to parents, siblings and friends. Since he cannot verbalize his feelings, he cannot achieve meaningful contacts with his environment. This often results in frustration, confusion, tension, despair and unusual behavior. The deaf child lives a life of constant anxious scrutiny by parents, physicians, friends and often teachers. He seldom knows how others regard him.

In addition to the historical background, the authors have seven chapters devoted to the deaf, their education, and social and vocational adjustment. In spite of the importance of the home, it is made clear to the reader that the parent is not a teacher and the home is not a formal classroom. Chapter II serves as a practical guide to parents and families of hearing impaired preschool children with direct suggestions regarding the disability and what to do about it. Suggestions are terse and to the point. The information regarding sources of help and information will be appreciated by parents, nurses, teachers and other professionals.

Some readers may be concerned that the publication is written from the standpoint of the residential school and reflects the philosophy of those who support such a facility. Obviously this is the climate with which the authors are familiar, and the stimulus of their story. In the chapter concerning information sources there are many suggestions for teaching language, English, reading, social studies, science and mathematics. The writers tell of the techniques that have worked successfully for them. Additional programs concerned with guidance, vocational training and placement and "extra-curricular" or recreational activities are described. Of special interest to many is the chapter on social development and dating. Those who are unfamiliar with the deaf will be surprised at the variety of jobs which they have performed successfully. Price in accomplishments is tempered by the realization that many needs and goals are still unmet.

Chapters IV and V will be of special interest to parents. The authors stress that deafness *does* make a child different. Parents and others should not treat the deaf child as though he had no problem or as though he were just like other children in the family, when it is so evident that he has serious differences. Under Chapter VI the historical background of psychological testing and the dangers and injustices which are prominent in the testing of the deaf are described clearly and frankly. The results of research at the Iowa school will be of special interest to psychologists and counselors. Chapter VII deals with the application of the seven cardinal principles of education to the deaf. In this section the authors present an interesting and startling contrast in the educational achievements of a hearing child and a deaf child.

In their conclusions the authors give a frank picture of the limitations of the deaf in comparison with the hearing. Giangrecos stress the need for more research resulting in more effective techniques and usable media. They plead for better understanding. This publication is the authors' way of helping others to help the Deaf.

MARSHALL S. HISKEY

PREFACE

NOT LONG AGO NEWSPAPERS in Iowa carried on a campaign to tell the story of Iowa so that people and industry might become better acquainted with what the state has to offer and become attracted to it. By that time we had been residents in the state eight years and were aware of the fact that Iowa is indeed a "beautiful land of plenty."

Iowa is a beautiful fertile land between two rivers—the Missouri on the west and the Mississippi on the east. Iowa produces at least one-tenth of the nation's food. Iowa is populated with educated people who are friendly, intelligent and industrious. It has the highest literacy rate in the country.

Iowa is lovely to view. In winter there is snow; spring and summer vistas show a mantle of greens, and autumn blends into a spectacular array of color. The four seasons are well-balanced so that each time of year has its own pleasures.

Iowa has a great history with many attractions available to show how Iowa shared in the growth of our nation.

With the proud heritage Iowa provides it is a pleasure to call it home. Because of the available opportunities, we have been able to accept the challenge of our profession in the education of the deaf. We hope we have met the challenges in some small way, for we have learned and grown as the result of being here. We have written this book to share the opportunities that we have been so fortunate to receive here in the heart of America—Iowa.

JOE AND MARIANNE GIANGRECO

INTRODUCTION

THE MULTIPLICITIES in the education of the school age hearing impaired youth in the world today are as varied as anyone could possibly imagine. Never, in the history of deaf education have so many "tools of the trade" been available in such quantities. Not only are *things* at the teachers' fingertips, but fertile minds are expounding ideas through mass media so that there is constant mental stimulation for those professionals willing to avail themselves through the various media of communication that are so easily available today. Old techniques are viewed in the light of new concepts. New revelations can be tested by the firm foundations of the past.

What is today's goal in the education of the hearing impaired? Where are we going? What can we expect to achieve? How can we measure the fruits of our labors? What has the past given us that is too good to relinquish? What things of the past need to be discarded in favor of new ideas? These are the relevent questions of our times.

In trying to solve some of these problems we have been working diligently at the Iowa School for the Deaf in Council Bluffs. The school has been a challenge to us as opportunities have been put in our path at every turn. Study in preparation for a career has become more meaningful when applied to the realities of life. Experiences have returned us to the classroom and advanced readings to aid in the search for answers to the challenges before us. Many observations have been made. Many areas of thought remain unanswered. In the search for knowledge certain concrete facts have been revealed and more doors opened. Each person who becomes caught in the spell of any profession must feel much the same way as the progression of time continues the pursuit of the curious.

In this book we have sought to combine facts and the ideas of others with our ideas and observations. Hopefully, the result will be a useful volume that will open the road of curiosity for others. Perhaps they, too, can accept the challenge of the education of the hearing impaired and contribute to the welfare of our nation and world in some way so the education of the hearing impaired may continue to progress with enthusiasm, and greater acruity. The lives of the students with impaired hearing must proceed to enriched adulthood of unsurpassed quality.

J. G.
M. G.

ACKNOWLEDGMENTS

THE FOLLOWING have assisted in many ways to make this publication possible and their help is greatly appreciated: Mrs. Graham Jennings, Mrs. Harold Parker, and The Iowa School for the Deaf Staff.

The following have given permission for the quotations used in this book:

"The Story of Lip Reading" Fred DeLand, Copyright 1931 and 1968 (c) by the Alexander Graham Bell Association for the Deaf, Washington, D. C.

"The Deaf and Their Problems" Kenneth Hodgson, Copyright 1953, Philosophical Library, New York City.

"The Conquests of Deafness" Ruth Bender, Copyright 1960, Western Reserve University Press, Cleveland, Ohio.

"Teaching The New Social Studies in Secondary Schools" Edwin Fenton, Copyright 1966, Holt, Rinehart and Winston, Inc., Chicago, Illinois.

"Voice of the Deaf" Maxine T. Boatner, Copyright 1959, Public Affairs Press, Washington, D. C.

"Social Studies: A Promise of a Better Tomorrow" C. Joseph Giangreco, Proceedings of International Conference on Oral Education of the Deaf, Vol. 1, p. 1803, Copyright 1967 (c) by the Alexander Graham Bell Association for the Deaf, Washington, D. C.

"Teaching English to Teenagers" C. Joseph and Marianne R. Giangreco, Volta Review, Vol. 59, p. 437, Copyright 1957 (c) by the Alexander Graham Bell Association for the Deaf, Washington, D. C.

CONTENTS

	Page
Foreword—Marshall S. Hiskey	vii
Preface	xi
Introduction	xiii
Acknowledgments	xv

Chapter

I. HISTORICAL BACKGROUND	3
II. PRESCHOOL CONSIDERATIONS	31
III. EDUCATING YOUTH	49
IV. POST-SCHOOL THOUGHTS	115
V. SPREADING KNOWLEDGE TO PARENTS AND THE PUBLIC	122
VI. PSYCHOLOGICAL ASPECTS	130
VII. PROFESSIONAL HINTS	150
VIII. CONCLUSIONS	166
Bibliography	173
Index	177

THE EDUCATION
OF THE
HEARING IMPAIRED

Chapter I

HISTORICAL BACKGROUND

ANCIENT GREEKS AND EARLY CHRISTIANS

The passage of hearing . . . ends at the place where the innate spiritus causes, on some animals, the pulsation of the heart, and in others, respiration; wherefore also it is that we are able to understand and repeat what we have heard, for as was the movement which entered through the sense organ, such again is the movement which is caused by means of the voice, being, as it were, of one and the same stamp, so that a man can say what he has heard.

Those who are born deaf all become senseless and incapable of reason. Men that are born deaf are in all cases dumb; that is to say, they can make vocal noises but they cannot speak . . . . Children, just as they have no control over other parts, so have no control at first over the tongue, but it is so far imperfect and only frees and detaches itself by degrees, so that in the interval children mostly lisp and stutter. (Hodgson, 1953, pp. 61-62)

T HE WORLD'S CONSCIOUSNESS of the hearing-handicapped began with these thoughts from Aristotle (384-322 B.C.). Aristotle's misconception held the fate of the deaf in its grasp for approximately 2,000 years. The transition from Aristotle to the present is a vast step. Only in relationship to the past can the present be appreciated. Therefore, it is noteworthy to review the steps of the past which make the modern concept of deaf education the threshold of relevance for the future.

Today, thought in the field of deaf education supports the concept that the deaf are not only people or children who cannot hear, but also, they are a minority group of individuals in our society. Although it is not initially obvious, deaf people differ from the general public in many ways. Helmer Myklebust (1953) points out the need for a "new understanding" of deafness. His research is concerned with the many possible differences that may exist between the deaf and the general public. The deaf

3

may have different maturation rates, intellectual composition and senses of sight and smell.

How have such concepts come into being? In prehistoric times living was not particularly easy, but it was characterized by simplicity. The family was the primary unit and this small group had to meet only the basic physical needs. To better satisfy these needs families banded together into small roaming groups. Each group member provided aid for distressed members and contributed to the common defense.

A type of simple culture evolved in these groups. Children had only to grow into adulthood, and take their parents' places in the tribe or group. In order to survive, a handicapped child was forced to succeed without special attention. Where the hearing-handicapped found their fate is not known, but certainly some must have survived.

Civilization acquired complexities, and as they multiplied more intricate laws were required. Old Testament references are among the earliest that pertain to the deaf. The Hebrews (500 B.C.) had laws protecting the deaf. Leviticus (19:14) states, "Thou shalt not curse the deaf, nor put a stumbling block before the blind, but shall fear thy God." The Old Testament laws must have resulted from persecution of the handicapped. It would seem only natural that the Jews should be among the first to be concerned about God's children and seek more humane treatment of the handicapped, for the Jewish religious concepts embrace close family relationships.

Pliny (77 A.D.) in his *History* says, "When one is first of all denied hearing, he is also robbed of the power of talking, and there are no persons born deaf who are not also dumb." (Farrar, 1923, pp. 1-2)

Later the Romans put forth laws concerning the deaf. The legal rights of the deaf were included in the Justinian Code (530 A.D.) as follows:

> 1. The deaf and dumb in whom both infirmities were present from birth: these were without legal rights or obligations. Guardians appointed for them by law were to have complete charge of their affairs.
>
> 2. Those who became deaf and dumb from causes arising after birth: if these people had acquired a knowledge of letters before

their affliction, they were allowed to conduct their own affairs by means of writing. This included marriage contracts, which were denied the previous class.

3. Those deaf from birth, but not dumb.

4. Those deaf from causes arising after birth, but not dumb: these two classes were assumed to have the use of language to a sufficient degree to carry on the responsibilities of their own lives. No restrictions seem to have been placed on their legal rights. They would undoubtedly be classified today as the hard of hearing and deafened.

5. Those who were dumb only, either from birth or from later causes: this classification is obscure. No restrictions were placed on these people, since it was assumed they could understand spoken language and reply in writing.

The law expressly stated that no discrimination was to be made between men and women in the administration of these rules. (Bender, 1960, pp. 23-24)

These laws were a step forward from the Spartan view that imperfect children should be permitted to die of over-exposure. It must be noted that in early times society had little place for any kind of handicapped person and often their presence presented an economic calamity. The Spartan viewpoint was not entirely out of place in its time.

The rise of Christianity (30 A.D.) was the beginning of meaningful philosophical change towards the deaf. Although the church accepted the thinking of Aristotle and excluded the deaf from church membership, Christianity's more kindly attitude towards all men benefited the deaf. Exclusion from the church was based on Romans 10:17 which says, "So faith comes from what is heard."

St. Augustine (354-430) wrote, ". . . from what source of culpability does it come that innocent ones deserve to be born sometimes blind, sometimes deaf, which defect, indeed, hinders faith itself, by the witness of the Apostle who says 'Faith comes by hearing.' (Bender, 1960, p. 27)

The ways of God were not to be questioned. The deaf were considered beyond human help and only divine miracles could alleviate their affliction. Mark 7:30-37 relates one of Jesus' miracles as follows:

Then he returned from the region of Tyre, and went through Sidon to the Sea of Galilee, through the region of the Decapolis. And they brought to him a man who was deaf and had an impediment in his speech; and they besought him to lay his hand upon him. And taking him aside from the multitude privately, he put his fingers into his ears, and he spat and touched his tongue; and looking up to heaven, he sighed, and said to him, 'Ephphatha,' that is, 'Be opened.' And his ears were opened, his tongue was released, and he spoke plainly. And he charged them to tell no one; but the more he charged them, the more zealously they proclaimed it. And they were astonished beyond measure, saying, 'He has done all things well; he even makes the deaf hear and the dumb speak.'

SIXTEENTH CENTURY

It was in the sixteenth century that the door opened toward enlightenment—and then only a beginning was established. In Italy a doctor by the name of Giralamo Cardano (1501-1576) made brief mention of the fact that he could see no reason why the deaf could not be taught. He did not pursue the matter, but this was in variance with the thinking of Aristotle which was the accepted code of the day. In the book, *Paralipomenom*, Cardano wrote the following,

> Agricola relates in his *De inventione dialectica* (published 1538) that he had seen a man born deaf and dumb, who had learnt to read and write, so that he could express whatever he wished. Thus it is possible to place a deafmute in a position to hear by reading, and to speak by writing; for his memory leads him to understand, by reflection, that "bread," as written, signifies the thing which is eaten. He thus reads, by the light of his reason, as it were in a picture; for by this means, though nothing is referred to sounds, not only objects, but actions and results are made known. And just as after seeing a picture, we may draw another picture guided simply by a conception of the objects represented, such is also the case with letters. For as different sounds are conventionally used to signify different things, so also may the various figures of objects and words. (Farrar, 1923, pp. 5-6) . . . The deaf were capable of reason: A revolutionary comment. (Bender, 1960, pp. 32-33)

The other spark of light in the sixteenth century flickered in Spain; deaf children were born to some of the nobility. In order for these children to inherit their just rights as nobility it was necessary for them to be educated. To retain the family standards, the Velasco family of the Constable of Castille sought a teacher for their deaf children, Francisco and Pedro. The challenge was taken by Pedro Ponce de Leon (1520-1584). Apparently de Leon was successful for the children were not forced to relinquish their legal rights. Records of de Leon's methods and accomplishments were destroyed in a monastery fire. It is generally agreed, however, that Ponce de Leon began his teachings with writing and progressed to speech.

Martin Luther (1483-1546) is supposed to have known of a deaf person who could attend religious services because he could "understand through the eye." (Deland, 1931, p. 42)

SEVENTEENTH CENTURY

With the pathway opened, the seventeenth century spurred interest in education. Intellectual growth took place in many areas, and the foundation of deaf education was made firm.

To appreciate what took place in direct relation to the deaf it is necessary to see what the philosophers were thinking. John Amos Comenius (1592-1671) said, "Things come before words, and symbols are of little use until the child has first had the experience which the symbols represent." (Bender, 1960, p. 49) Comenius felt that children should be taught what they want to learn, and that the entirety of a concept is a summary of its parts. John Locke (1632-1704) felt that sense training was a primary step in education. The concept of sense training was a turning point in educational thought and a boon for the handicapped. Francis Bacon (1561-1626) advocated the use of experimentation. Realism became a basic principal of learning.

Practical applications of these ideas were negligible. Some of the more fortunate rich were educated, including some of the deaf. Cardano's ideas were examined with some benefit for the deaf.

Juan Pablo Bonet (1579-1629), another Spaniard, described the progress of the education of the deaf in his book, "*Simplification of the Alphabet and the Method of Teaching Deaf-Mutes to Speak*" (1620). This was the literary foundation stone of deaf education. "Bonet was out to secure language for the deaf by any means at first," says Kenneth Hodgson, "by gesture or sign, teaching at the same time the alphabet in writing."

> Then his plan was to teach the sounds in association with the letters. He would have his pupils memorize the printed alphabet, the manual alphabet, and the associated sounds, commencing with the vowels. Then they were to acquire a working vocabulary of nouns, and then of verbs. Next came the abstract nouns in association with the states of qualities concerned, which were to be artificially produced or simulated. With abstract nouns conveniently mastered, the teacher was to pass on to conjunctions, adverbs, prepositions, which were to be learned by heart.
>
> Bonet's work commanded attention not only in Spain, but also outside. He realized that mental development is language, nothing less, nothing more; and that the first duty of a teacher is to secure that development by any means at his disposal, using signs and gestures so long as they are necessary, and useful, dropping them only as wholly verbal language, either spoken, written or spelled on the fingers, becomes adequate for the pupil's purposes.
>
> There is thus a development on de Leon, whose sole aim was speech, with the mental development really incidental . . . . . [Bonet] sought not only speech, but complete education, and was the first to make deliberate use of lip-reading for a pupil. (Hodgson, 1953, pp. 94-95)

Bonet taught Don Luis de Valesco, an adept pupil. At a wedding in Spain in 1623 Valesco met Sir Kenelm Digby (1603-1665) of England. This relationship influenced the spread of deaf education to England. Digby was so impressed with Bonet's student that years later he wrote of Valesco in a book published in England (1646):

> The Spanish lord was born deaf; so deaf that if a gun were shot off close by his ear, he could not hear it; and consequently, he was dumb; for not being able to hear the sound of words, he could neither imitate nor understand them. The loveliness of his face, and especially the exceeding life and spiritfulness of his eyes, and the comliness of his person and whole composure of his body throughout, were pregnant signs of a well-tempered mind within. And therefore all that knew him lamented much the want of means to cultivate it, to which remedy physicians and chirurgeons had long employed their skill; but all in vain. At the last there was a priest who undertook teaching him to understand others when they spoke, and to speak himself that others might understand him. What at the first he was laughed at for, made him after some years be looked

upon as if he had wrought a miracle. In a word, after strange patience, constancy, and pains, he brought the young lord to speak as distinctly as any man whosoever; and to understand so perfectly what others said that he would not lose a word in a whole day's conversation.

He could discern in another, whether he spoke shrill or low, and he would repeat after anybody any hard word whatsoever. Which the Prince tried often; not only in English, but by making some Welshmen that served his Highness speak words of their language which he so perfectly echoed that I confess I wondered more at that than at all the rest. And his master himself would acknowledge that the rules of his art reached not to produce that effect with any certainty. And therefore concluded this in him must spring from other rules he had framed unto himself, out of his own attentive observation; which, the advantage that nature had just given him in the sharpness of his other senses, to supply the want of this; endowed him with an ability and sagacity to do, beyond any other man that had his hearing. He expressed it surely in a high measure of his so exact imitation of the Welch pronounciation; for that tongue, like the Hebrew, employeth much the gutteral letters . . . He could converse currently in the light, though they he talked with whispered ever so softly. And I have seen him at the distance of a large chamber's breadth say words after one that I standing close by the speaker could not hear a syllable of. But if he were in the dark, or if one turned his face out of his sight, he was capable of nothing one said. (Deland, 1931, pp. 35-37)

Dr. John Bulwer (1614-1684) was the first Englishman to write at length on deafness. His interest in the deaf was ignited by Digby's book. Bulwer was aware of the problems of the deaf before Digby, but Bonet, through Digby, was the spark that spurred Bulwer into activity. Through his books Bulwer brought knowledge of help for the deaf to England. He mentioned that a school for the deaf might be advisable and commented that he felt dumbness was not a necessary effect of deafness.

The quarrel between Dr. John Wallis (1617-1703) and Dr. William Holder (1616-1698) concerning the best method of teaching the deaf created public interest in deafness. Holder did not succeed as a teacher at first, and Wallis was considered a successful instructor. They had a mutual pupil who failed under Holder and learned under Wallis. The quarrel in itself was unimportant historically, but the fact that it created news and made the public aware of a group of handicapped people in their midst provided valuable publicity at the time the quarrel occurred.

Two other Englishmen who added to the literary aspects of deafness were Meric Casaubon (1665) and Daniel Defoe (1660-1731). Casaubon wrote a book in which he said,

> by the perfect knowledge whereof the deaf and dumb may be taught not only to understand whatever is spoken by others; as some (upon credible information) have done in England; but also to speak and to discourse. (Deland, 1931, p. 60)

He told of several people who were speechreaders. He recommended speechreading for the hearing, as well as the deaf, when the use of voice would be disturbing.

Defoe, of *Robinson Crusoe* fame, published a book entitled, *The History of the Life and Adventures of Mr. Duncan Campbell,* "a gentleman, who though deaf and dumb, writes down any stranger's name at first sight with their future contingencies of fortune. Now living in Exeter, over against the Savoy in the Strand."

The book was ficticious, but was written so realistically that the readers never doubted the novel's authenticity. The book made reference to the capabilities of the deaf. Mr. Duncan and these "capabilities" spread far and wide through the book's popularity.

Also in Great Britain, George Dalgarno (1626-1687) of Scotland, expounded the merits of manual alphabets and even developed one. Dalgarno spurred the development of language when he wrote, " . . . let occasions be the best mistress of method." (Farrar, 1923, p. 25). It was years before his efforts were appreciated.

Francis Mercurius, the Baron von Helmont (1618-1699) of Belgium fancied the idea that mystical language study would reveal unusual truths previously unknown. He used the mystical approach in teaching a deaf girl to talk. Von Helmont felt that there must be a return to a base language and that this language was Hebrew. Von Helmont's accomplishments are shrouded in skepticism. Though his approach is unorthodox, he did achieve some success.

Johann Konrad Amman (1669-1724), born in Switzerland, was voluntarily exiled to Holland because of his religious beliefs. He was a firm advocate of speech and speechreading. Amman developed several techniques for instructing the deaf. Among the methods about which Amman wrote was this: "I put their hand to my throat and command them to imitate me." (Hodgson, 1953, p. 105)

Amman's method included the following:

1. They who hear with such difficulty that they can neither frequent the house of prayer, nor the society of their friends without feeling real inconvenience, may so exercise themselves before a mirror that, in spite of their deafness, they may learn to hear with their eyes and derive the greatest pleasure from the exercise.

2. Boys under a skillful teacher may not only learn to read whatever language they please by this method in an incredible short time, but may also learn to pronounce every language which they acquire, if while learning, they accustom themselves to attend to the formation of each letter.

3. They will afterwards hear with their eyes as well as their ears, and by this means they will frequently obtain a great advantage; for we are often much concerned by what is done or said secretly of us, and by what is clandestinely plotted against us or other people, which though we were present might easily be concealed by muttering with a low voice; happy should we be if, by detecting with the eyes what was denied to the ears, we could escape danger, and find out in this way the insidious secrets of others. (Deland, 1931, pp. 65-66)

Hodgson summarizes the seventeenth century very well when he says:

The century had opened with no more than a story of Agricolas, a few remarks of Cardano, and the unique teaching of the Spanish priest, Ponce de Leon. But by the close there was a literature on the subject, records of successful teaching in four countries, and a widespread recognition of the possibilities of teaching speech and speechreading. Miracles had become practical: something to be accepted as quite within the ordinary bounds of human achievement. On this much stronger foundation the next century was to build. (Hodgson, 1953, p. 106)

EIGHTEENTH CENTURY

A social consciousness of human suffering developed during the eighteenth century. The wealthy had ignored the poor, but with the arrival of the eighteenth century the wealthy felt a need to aid them. The poor deaf became recognized; schools were opened, humanitarianism came to light, but medical help continued to remain an almost untouched field.

Drama, evidenced the traditional accepted feeling toward the deaf. Oliver Goldsmith (1728-1774) portrayed a deaf man as an object of ridicule in one of his plays.

Germany developed a state school system for the deaf. Austria, Saxony and Prussia began state schools for the deaf. English schools for the deaf were available only to the wealthy.

Mary Wollstonecraft (1792) wrote about teaching methods in her book, *Vindication of the Rights of Women:*

> How much time is lost in teaching [the deaf] to recite what they do not understand . . . . Yet how can these things be remedied when school masters depend entirely on parents for subsistence? . . . Little exertion can be expected of them, more than is necessary to please ignorant people. Indeed, the necessity of giving the parents some sample of the boys' abilities is productive of more mischief than would at first be supposed. For it is seldom done entirely by the child . . . and thus the master countenances a falsehood . . . and the memory is overloaded with unintelligible words to make a show of. (Hodgson, 1953, p. 115)

Hodgson felt that this description was especially perceptive of the situation for the deaf in the eighteenth century. During this time children were considered miniature adults. Little consideration was given to their own activities and interest. The child was required to fit the style of his school situation just as he fit his clothing. Quoting Hodgson:

> We do know that a few deaf children from wealthy homes were taught, but when we consider the terrible prevalence of fevers we can only conclude that most of the rich who had children were so ashamed and mortified at the circumstance that the Calibans were kept from public view. In Catholic countries it was the practice to immure them in monasteries and convents. But English Society disposed of its afflicted young even more shamefacedly, considering that if the creature's wants were satisfied that was all that was reasonably fitting. (Hodgson, 1953, p. 115)

Despite all these aspects of the problems of the deaf, the

deaf child was not always at a tremendous disadvantage until mid-eighteenth century when society began losing its characteristic simplicity. Machines began to appear. They were more difficult to explain or understand by sight only. The world was suddenly progressing, and the deaf were being left behind. The world was moving faster than the teacher of the deaf could teach and no new methods of instruction were available. Teachers of the deaf were at work, though, and there were several who stand out in this period.

In England, Henry Baker (1698-1774) saw a relative's eight-year-old deaf daughter and became interested in her welfare. She became his first pupil after he familiarized himself with Daniel Defoe's ficticious account of Duncan Campbell. Dr. Wallis' methods were also known to Baker. Essentially, Baker used speech and speechreading as his approach. He claimed to have improved upon Wallis' method. Apparently Baker's work was very successful among his selected pupils. His work, or rather his particular methods, were kept secret for business reasons.

Baker was one of the first men to attempt to gain a livelihood solely by teaching the deaf. Previous teachers had done so as an avocation. The aura of secrecy surrounding methods of instructing the deaf began with Baker and prevailed until recent times.

Jacob Rodriguez Pereira (1715-1780), a Spanish Jew, received recognition as probably the first teacher of the deaf in France. He successfully taught his deaf sister and soon acquired other pupils because of this early success. His methods were secret, but he was so successful as a teacher that he was called, "the greatest teacher of them all." (Hodgson, 1953, p. 121) Pereira won acclaim from the French Academy of Science and was elected a fellow of the Royal Society. Upon his death some of his ideas were made available. Among this natural teacher's techniques, Hodgson points out the following:

> Pereira relied on the one-handed Spanish alphabet, though with improvements of his own. He also employed a battery of signs, but these were dispensed with as verbal language became adequate through speech, reading, and lipreading. All the time the pupil

went through a constant repetition of the mechanical speech exercises. Then as speech and lipreading grew stronger, vocabulary was increased by means of the question-and-answer system, using "live" language about matters of current interest. Diaries and letter-writing supplied the written practice.

What made Pereira was his innate genius, that brilliant intuition which showed him alone how most perfectly to make vision and touch supply the deficiencies of hearing. Buffon (1707-1788) wrote of his work: "Nothing could show more conclusively how much senses are alike at bottom and to what point they may supply one another." But no treatise on method could have made another teacher his equal. (Hodgson, 1953, pp. 122-123)

Jean Jacques Rousseau (1712-1788), the philosopher and writer, was a neighbor of Pereira's. He "thought highly of his [Pereira's] ingenuity in securing the natural development of language for the deaf." (Hodgson, 1953, p. 123)

Baker and Pereira appear to have established deaf education as a profession but it was for de l'Epee (1712-1789) to make deaf education a matter of public concern.

Charles Michael de l'Epee was well educated and destined for priesthood. At first he was denied his ambition, but later he was accepted into the priesthood and assigned to Paris, France. One day while visiting his parishioners, de l'Epee met two deaf twins. These sisters disturbed de l'Epee, and he worried about the fate of their souls because they could not know salvation. As a result, he decided to undertake the education of these twins so that they could receive church instruction. Before long he had a group of deaf followers,

. . . to teach them to think with order and to combine their ideas. This I thought I might succeed in doing by making use of representative signs reduced to a method of which I composed a kind of grammar. (Hodgson, 1953, p. 125)

When I took on the education of the two deaf and dumb sisters, it did not enter my head to teach them to speak. Charmed with the facility of teaching them to write, I did not think of untying their tongues. (Bender, 1960, p. 80)

Unlike previous teachers of the deaf de l'Epee was not secretive—a fact that was to play a major role in the future of deaf education, especially in the United States.

De l'Epee saw to it that his students remained happy. However, they were generally isolated from the world. This was partly due to his non-oral approach.

> For all that he was right in realizing with Cardano and Dalgarno, that spoken words are signs as arbitrary as any signs made with the hands, he had become prejudiced against speech. Some oralist teachers have succeeded in taking their pupils to the summit of thought by the very difficult path of artificially acquired speech. But de l'Epee had made up his mind that path led nowhere. Instead he shepherded his flock into a pleasant pasture where they could at least enjoy each other's company and his through the eye and the hand. But they could not delight in anyone else's thought because the signs they used were a private language. We cannot doubt but that the children he fostered were vastly more happy, though, in their secluded alp or mountain of thought than they were in the dark valleys of abysmal untrained, uncared for ignorance. If they could never know the summit, at least they were high up in the sun. (Hodgson, 1953, p. 127)

> As his work progressed, the Abbe became convinced that the signs the deaf made with their hands in trying to communicate with each other were the basis of a mother tongue for them, in much the same way that one's native language is for a hearing person. He set himself to expand and elaborate these signs, in order to develop them into full language, capable of expressing abstract thought, as well as concrete ideas in pantomime. He did not condemn the efforts of others in teaching articulation, but since, in his opinion, the deaf were capable of thought and reason only in the use of signs, he could see no purpose for speech. To him, even writing, was for the deaf, a translation from the sign language. (Bender, 1960, p. 81)

> Unfortunately a manual sign language in very restricted use degenerates faster than other kinds of language in more widespread use. The signer has gradually a smaller and smaller battery of signs, each coming with usage to convey more and more meanings, but less meaning, because precision is lost. But we are not entitled to boast too much of the conceptional rigidity of our ordinary language, which can degenerate to such vague noun-substitutes as "the what-d'you-call-it" and "the what's-its-name." Language obeys the law of degeneration and diminution among the hearing just as it does among the deaf using manual language. (Hodgson, 1953, p. 129)

De l'Epee's work received much recognition. The king even provided funds for his work. Aside from teaching and running his school, de l'Epee increased his devotion to the deaf by writing about his work. In addition to writing books he carried on a correspondence with Samuel Heinicke of Germany which is very noteworthy.*

"The direct link of influence on American schools for the deaf was from the Abbe de l'Epee. The Abbe Roch Ambroise Cucurron Sicard (1742-1882) successfully carried on the work in France both before and after the French Revolution. He was followed by Roch Ambroise Auguste Bebain (1789-1839) who had as his assistant Laurent Clerc (1785-1869), the man who accompanied Thomas Hopkins Gallaudet to the United States to set up schools in the United States."

In Germany de l'Epee's contemporary, Samuel Heinicke (1727-1790), was formulating his teaching techniques and after attempts in several fields finally found himself and took charge of a deaf school where he became seriously interested in teaching. Heinicke remained secretive about his work except in letters he wrote to de l'Epee. Since Heinicke was very successful in his teaching and formed what was to be the major foundation for the oral philosophy in deaf teaching, these letters assume importance. Heinicke could see no possible compromise between speech and signs. Heinicke was learned and well-informed about the philosophy of his day. He felt that breadth of interest was essential to success.

Heinicke's method . . . was essentially intuitive. For Heinicke, experience had to precede words. At first he used reading and writing before speech, and only in the second phase of his career did he reverse the process, teaching speech from the outset and using writing only to fix ideas acquired orally. But always he used pictures and mimic gestures to assist understanding. (Hodgson, 1953, p. 137)

Heinicke said "Work is the basis of modern oral teaching." He contended that the manual alphabet and signs have their dangers if speech is the aim. Many of Heinicke's predecessors had seen these manual devices as a crutch to assist the deaf in walking mentally. It was left to Heinicke to argue that a crutch may itself be a handicap to those who have never walked, because it can make them disinclined to try. The only way to learn to speak is to speak. "The deaf mute can learn and should be taught to speak," Heinicke declared, "and language as spoken should be the instrument of instruction and . . . by such means will the unhappy one be restored to Society." (Hodgson, 1953, p. 138)

Heinicke's two strongest convictions were that

1. Clear thought is possible only by speech, and, therefore, the deaf ought to be taught to speak.
2. The deaf can understand the speech of another from the motion of the lips. (Deland, 1931, p. 86)

His ultimate goal was that deaf education should not segregate the deaf for happiness, but rather make them happy members of society at large.

On continental Europe, two distinct methods evolved—manual and oral. Not only were these associated with the deaf, but with national boundaries and religious differences as well. The stage was set for a political football match that still exists worldwide.

While all this was happening on the continent, Great Britain witnessed the emergence of an outstanding teacher, Thomas Braidwood. Like Germany's Heinicke, Braidwood (1715-1806) was a natural teacher and an oralist, who was secretive in his work. Because of the success of his teaching Braidwood advertised by letters in a magazine. Through these and other accounts that became known, Braidwood's method seemed to be as follows:

He pronounces the sound "a" slowly, pointing out the figure of the letter at the same time; makes his pupil observe the motion of his mouth and throat; he then puts his fingers into his pupil's mouth, depresses or elevates his tongue, and makes him keep the part in that position; and then he lays hold of the outside of the windpipe and gives some kind of squeeze which is impossible to describe . . . . the pupil is anxiously imitating him, but at first seems not to understand what he would have him to do. In this manner he proceeds till the pupil has learned to pronounce all the sounds. (Hodgson, 1953, p. 146)

Another account gives this information:

There is one subject of philosophical curiosity to be found in Edinburgh which no other city has to show; a college of the deaf and dumb, who are taught to read, to speak, to write, to practice arithmetic by a gentleman whose name is Braidwood. The number which attends him is, I think, about twelve which he brings together into a little school. . . . The improvement of Mr. Braidwood's pupils is wonderful. They not only speak, write, and understand what is written, but if he that speaks looks towards them and modifies his organs by full and distinct utterance they know so well what is spoken that it is an expression scarcely figurative to say that they hear with the eyes. (Hodgson, 1953, p. 147)

It was most pleasing to see one of the most desperate of human calamities capable of so much help: whatever enlarges hope will exalt courage; after having seen the deaf taught arithmetic, who would be afraid to cultivate the Hebrides? (Farrar, 1923, p. 67)

The eighteenth century had been one of increasing advancement and growth with mass education for the deaf. It became reality under de l'Epee with his manual approach, and with selective education along oral lines realized under both Heinicke and Braidwood. The inspiration to do work for and with the deaf became worldwide in scope as a result of the work done by the outstanding men of the eighteenth century. Although the schools that resulted left much to be desired by today's standards the fact that many became a reality in the nineteenth century and that the desire to do something became widespread certainly are accomplishments to be given consideration in the history of deaf education.

Johann Heinrich Pestalozzi (1746-1827) and Friedrich Froebel (1782-1852) possessed distinct ideas on education. They expressed their ideas publicly but were ignored. Froebel's kindergarten concept was shortlived in his day; the need to make children self-reliant through well-trained teachers was not agreeable to the rulers of the time. For "children to be free to do, free to move and free to be themselves in tune with the teacher" (Hodgson, 1953, p. 1953) is still an unreached goal in total, but Pestalozzi and Froebel were working hard for its beginning.

Froebel's book, *The Education of Man,* (1826) expresses the idea that a child's growth is "the unfolding of one of Nature's plans" (Hodgson, 1953, p. 153) and man should not force a man-made plan upon the child nor should this lead to an opposite pole that there is no plan needed at all (untended and untrained children). Rather his idea was that the plan of Nature must be watched and interpreted so that it can be enhanced.

The 1800's saw practically nothing done in the way of hearing devices, even though medicine was out of the witchcraft state. There were names for the parts of the hearing mechanism. Certain operations were available for the middle ear, and research was probing the semicircular canals.

Dr. Jean Marc Gaspard Itard (1774-1838) of Paris did some research into the heredity aspects of deafness. Although he did not reach a full understanding of deafness, he did show that it could be inherited. Itard's conclusions were as follows: (1) Deafness often skips one or more generations. (2) Deafness is not sex related, and (3) deafness followed the principle of Mendel's Laws. In addition to this work in medical research Itard offered much more to deaf education than was realized until more recently.

As a physician in a school for the deaf in Paris, Itard undertook the education of a wild boy—The Wild Boy of Aveyron. (1799) In working with this initially less than human boy, Itard felt that he could prove that environmental changes could completely restore the child to normalcy in society. Although he made astronomical improvement in Victor, the child never was truly restored to society, and Itard felt that his work was a total failure. Itard's work with Victor was the stimulus for beginning work with the mentally retarded. Itard and his followers, Edward Seguin (1812-1880) and Marie Montessori, (1870) contributed much towards the present philosophies in all areas of education because of their efforts to educate those considered less than normal.

NINETEENTH CENTURY

After Itard, Edouard Seguin (1812-1880) continued probing the relationship of science to education—especially handicapped children—and the following are some of his main principles.

1. That senses can be submitted to training, by which their capacity may be intellectualized.

2. That one sense can take the place of another as a means of intellectual comprehension and culture.

3. That sensations are intellectual functions performed through external (i.e. end-organ) apparatus.

4. That the education of the senses therefore prepares pabulum for the mind.

5. That education is not the putting into action of already acquired faculties, but the development of functions and aptitudes through the training of the senses . . . through incessant provocation in action (i.e. that education is active response to situations). (Hodgson, 1953, p. 192)

Tuning forks were developed as a test of refinement in the making of steel. They were later found to be useful as a means of testing hearing. Two theories of hearing evolved. Hermann von Helmholtz (1821-1894) conceived of a resonance theory (1863) which attempted to explain how hearing takes place by sound activating a response due to resonators in the inner ear. This theory made a distinction between deaf and hard-of-hearing people, a refinement heretofore not made. The telephone theory of hearing was developed in 1865 by Rinne, a German physicist. Rinne felt that the ear, including the inner ear, was only a transmitter of sound to the brain.

Literature and drama kept the public aware of deafness. Beethoven (1770-1827) was a public wonder as he continued to compose music in spite of his hearing loss.

In England Joseph Watson (1765-1829) set the pace of headmasters of asylums for the deaf. Headmasters were, from the beginning, men of assured income and social position. They saw little of their children. The assistants who lived with and taught the children were their charges year in and year out and certainly must have been dedicated people.

If at times they were themselves cruel, who dare criticize them? In that unrelenting, unrelieved atmosphere of horrible habits and barbarious noises, of long toil for but slight satisfaction and reward, we may well wonder that any of them retained their sanity. They were indeed poor devils; but they deserve the gratitude of posterity for what they did. (Hodgson, 1953, p. 159)

The Braidwoods and the Watsons operated nearly all early English asylums. The first Braidwood was a talented teacher and the rest lived on his laurels. Watson based the operation of his school on his predecessors, the Braidwoods. Watson had no use for sign language, and like Heinicke, he felt a great compulsion toward speech.

Would it not be a more natural and rational mode of procedure (he asked) for the teacher to begin by watching the objects and occasions to which the scholar applied the words of his barbarous speech; that by knowing these he might gradually substitute the words of the language to be taught; using the former only as an introduction to the latter? (Hodgson, 1953, p. 160)

In 1822 the adult deaf decided to help themselves through the establishment of a city mission to the adult deaf in Glasgow, Scotland. This was the beginning of a system of welfare help in which there is a social outlet as well as guidance for the post-school deaf person. This system still exists in Great Britain.

At this time French deaf education was under the direction of Sicard, and enthusiasm seemed to be waning somewhat in that country. However, the French continued to expound their ideas and spread them abroad. Hence, France was recognized as a leader by other nations even though her own vigor was lessening.

In 1817 Denmark had compulsory education for the deaf from ages eight to sixteen years. Finland and Russia opened schools for the deaf in 1840. In Germany Johann Baptiste Graeser (1765-1841) tried to put deaf children into public schools after two years of special training. His project did not work out but he is given credit for trying something different. Graeser recognized that the asylum system, as it was then functioning, was not satisfactory and he was willing to try something else.

Fredrick Moritz Hill (1805-1874), a student of Graeser, became one of the greatest teachers of this period. He taught in the school founded by Heinicke. Hill was an advocate of the "mother method" of Pestalozzi.

The "mother method," according to Pestalozzi, was the method of acquiring knowledge, as it was used between an infant and his mother, simply by normal, natural, repeated everyday contact with the things involved in daily living. (Bender, 1960, p. 133)

Hill wrote a great deal for publication and his thinking is revealed through his writing. Hill was willing to talk where others had been secretive. Ruth Bender sums up his work in three principles:

1. Deaf children should be taught language in the same way

that hearing children learn it, by constant daily use, associated with the proper objects and actions. As an aid to this, Hill designed a set of charts, each containing sixteen colored pictures, and supplemented by a series of special readers.

2. Speech must be the basis of all language, as it is with hearing children. Therefore, oral language must be taught before reading and writing. His lessons featured simple, but natural, conversation between teacher and child, and between child and child.

3. Speech must be used from the beginning as a basis for teaching and communication. Hill did not exclude the use of natural gestures as a means of understanding, but felt that they could rapidly be replaced by oral language. (Bender, 1960, p. 133)

Of natural gestures Hill says:

To banish the use of natural signs from our classrooms would be like excluding from ordinary schools the imperfect mother tongue of the hearing child. (Hodgson, 1953, p. 215)

Awaken in your pupils above all the feeling that language is a necessity for them, "and everything can be used for the teaching of language." (Hodgson, 1953, p. 216)

Only when language was mastered in use, both orally and in writing, did Hill introduce any formal teaching, bringing out grammar by use, and not by rule, making adroit use of his picture charts and whatever situations came to hand at the moment. He hoped thereby to make language a "lifelong study" for the children. And as a Pestalozzian, he knew that the basis of a lifelong study is intense interest. To whet this appetite for knowledge he taught at the child's speed and in tune with the unfolding plan of life. (Hodgson, 1953, pp. 216-217)

After this beautiful attempt at education, Johann Friedrich Herbart's (1776-1841) philosophy of formalism became a part of education and its misuse sidetracked the work of such teachers as Hill.

In the United States those deaf children who were educated were sent abroad—usually to England. The child of Francis Green (1780) was one of those who studied abroad. As a result Francis Green wrote of the deaf from his Massachusetts vantage point.

The Bolling family of Virginia was another family that had deaf children who studied abroad. Since they had several deaf children, they decided to bring a teacher to their home. This decision resulted in the hiring of John Braidwood, a grandson of Thomas Braidwood of English fame. John Braidwood could not overcome his personal shortcoming of alcoholism so his ability as a teacher remained questionable and the establishment of a school in Virginia was never accomplished. When Braidwood was released by the Bolling family, he went to New York to start a school; but his drunkenness interferred again. Thus, the schools for the deaf in this country did not begin with oral methods.

Another attempt to start a school for the deaf in the United States was undertaken by the Reverend John Stanford (1810). He was a chaplain at the Humane and Criminal Institutions of New York and he found deaf children within these places. He provided certain supplies for these children. Although Stanford began his efforts in 1810, it was not until 1818 that the New York Institution for the Deaf and Dumb (later known as the New York School for the Deaf) came into existence. (This was one year after the American Asylum opened under Gallaudet—the first school in this country.)

The father of deaf education in America was Thomas Hopkins Gallaudet (1787-1851). As the oldest of twelve children, Thomas attended school in Hartford, Connecticut, and graduated from Yale in 1805. Because of poor health he did not immediately seek employment. Instead he remained at home and studied English literature and law. He returned to Yale and after two years received his master of arts degree. With this background the lure of the new frontier beckoned and Gallaudet decided to become a trader and traveled as far as Kentucky.

Returning to Hartford in 1811, Gallaudet discovered that a new seminary had opened and he decided to return to school once more and to prepare himself for the ministry. In 1814 he was graduated.

Gallaudet, toward the conclusion of his schooling, became aware of nine-year-old Alice Cogswell, who had become deaf as the result of a fever. Being quite intrigued by the problem of educating such a child, Gallaudet sought to teach her. Dr. Cogswell, Alice's father, added to Gallaudet's enthusiasm by giving him a book he had secured from France. All of this culminated in a realization that there must be many children who

needed special education due to deafness. Dr. Cogswell sought
the help of friends in the community and then suggested that
Gallaudet go abroad to learn how to teach the deaf. Startled as
he was by the proposal, Gallaudet accepted. In May of 1815
Gallaudet sailed for England.

> In England and Scotland he was bitterly disappointed to find
> that the teaching of the deaf was a monopoly confined to the Braid-
> wood family; and there was neither the money nor the time to serve
> the years of apprenticeship required. Fortunately, while in London,
> he met Abbe Sicard, who invited him to Paris as a guest of his in-
> stitution. Thomas had already seen enough of "method" in English
> classrooms to realize that the English concentrated on teaching the
> deaf to speak; from Sicard's textbook he knew that the French
> teachers relied upon the Abee de l'Epee's creation of a system of
> signs in which a "sign" stood for a word.
>
> When writing to his friend Dr. Cogswell, Thomas stated: "I
> should wish, and I yet hope, to combine the peculiar advantages of
> both the French and the English modes of instruction, for there are
> considerable differences between them." It is interesting to note that
> here for the first time he used the word "combine" in connection
> with the two methods. (Boatner, 1959, pp. 4-5)

Although the English ways were not available to Gallaudet,
he found the French schools opened for his appraisal. Gallaudet
learned their ideas, methods and techniques. When he was
ready to return home he brought Laurent Clerc (1785-1869)
with him to help establish state schools for the deaf based on
the French ideology. American education of the deaf came into
existence at Hartford, Connecticut, with the opening of the
American Asylum for the Deaf and Dumb in 1817. (It was later
renamed the American School for the Deaf.) Thomas Gallaudet
was head of the Asylum for thirteen years until his frail physical
condition demanded retirement from its strenuous duties. Gallaudet married Sophia Fowler, one of the first students of the
school. Gallaudet died in 1880 but his son Edward Miner furthered his father's achievements.

The opening of the Hartford school established the trend
for state schools for the deaf. The French philosophy, of which
Gallaudet was a proponent, was not to go uncontested even in
its initial stages. Horace Mann (1796-1859) was working in the

interest of public school education and in his travels abroad he noted the German and English results of oral education for the deaf. When he had an opportunity to do so he questioned Gallaudet's approach and was one of the first Americans to advocate the oral method of instruction in this country. Samuel Gridley Howe (1801-1876) of Perkins Institute for the Blind in Boston also questioned Gallaudet's ways. Howe was the first to teach a deaf-blind child.

A group of coincidences outside of the profession in the Boston area furthered oral education of the deaf in this country. In 1863 three little girls about four years of age had been deafened and were being taught separately and unknown to each other by teachers unaware of the efforts to teach the deaf in Hartford. All cases were using what would be termed an oral approach. Fanny Cushing was being tutored by Harriet Rogers, a former teacher of hearing children. Jeanie Lippitt was a scarlet fever victim whose mother was trying to teach her. Her father was the Governor of Rhode Island. The third girl was Mabel Hubbard, also a scarlet fever victim being taught by Mary True.

Gardiner Hubbard, Mabel's father, sought advice at Hartford and found it so repulsive that he later went to Samuel Gridley Howe who encouraged him to try having Mabel tutored with hearing children by Mary True. The influential Gardiner Hubbard was pretentious and soon the three girls and their families discovered each other. Their joint efforts battled against the influence of Gallaudet and in 1867 the philanthropist John Clarke made possible the establishment of an oral school for the deaf at Northampton, Massachusetts.

The pressure for speech was felt and the utilization of any hearing a person might have seemed advantageous. The work going on at the Clarke School for the Deaf became publicized and the oral concepts spread into other areas. A branch or additional school, the Boston School for Deaf Mutes, was established in Boston in 1869 but was renamed the Horace Mann School.

Into this setting appeared Alexander Graham Bell, who was to make a profound impact upon the future of deaf education. Bell's father was Alexander Melville Bell (1819-1905), an elocution professor at Edinburgh, Scotland. He was anxious to develop a universal language and developed what is known as the Bell Symbols. When poor health struck the family and Mrs. Bell's hearing waned, Alexander Melville moved his family to Canada. A speaking engagement in Boston on his Symbols caught the attention of the teachers at the Boston School for Deaf Mutes and they asked if Alexander Melville would visit the school and instruct them. He recommended his son, Alexander Graham, instead and that resulted in A. G. Bell's taking residence in Boston.

When the Hubbards heard of the new Mr. Bell, they sent Mabel to him for instruction. The family and Bell soon developed a close relationship. The Hubbards were instrumental in seeing that Bell's experiments were financed. The discovery of the telephone financed and established Bell's independence.

Bell's mother was deaf; Bell taught the deaf and then took Mabel Hubbard as his wife. It is thus understandable that Bell felt a very close tie to the education of the deaf and influenced it both in word and deed.

With money received from the Volta prize, given to him for the invention of the telephone, Bell made possible the Volta Bureau in Washington, D. C. which is a library and research center for deaf education. Out of this grew the Alexander Bell Association for the Deaf, a teacher-parent organization for the pursuance of oral education for the deaf. The discovery of the telephone laid the way for an electronic approach to aids for hearing. Bell saw the remarkable abilities of his wife and others who had received an oral education and chose to differ openly with Gallaudet on ways of educating the deaf. Bell was active in meetings of the deaf profession and was instrumental in making speech and speechreading a part of the programs of such meetings. In 1894 the American Association to Promote the Teaching of Speech to the Deaf met and had a section on speechreading. Letters were read from people who used this medium of communication and the outstanding one was given by Mabel Bell.

Speechreading, . . is the systematized result of practice:I. In selecting the right word from a large assortment of possible words presented to the eye. II. In the power of grasping the meaning of what is said as a whole, from possibly a few words, or from parts of those words recognized here and there.

There are a very large number of words which are alike to the eye . . . . It is necessary that there should be an intimate knowledge of a large number of words from which to select the probable word, and second, that the habit of making the selection should be so well established that it could be done instantaneously and automatically. In perfect speechreading there is no more conscious effort in this selection than in the act of winking.

In consequence of the large number of words that are alike to the eye, the art of speechreading consists in seeking to grasp the meaning of what is said as a whole, rather than in wasting time trying to decipher the words one by one. By making sure of a word, here and there, by the method shown above, the trained mind is able to fill the blanks between, and to spring instantaneously to a clear realization of what is being said.

With me, this training began from the very beginning, and the habit was formed unconsciously, and I am only made aware of its existence when struggling with the difficulty of understanding a stranger. I have no doubt, however, that this habit could be systematically cultivated. It should not take long for one possessing a good knowledge of language and a quick bright mind to develop into a fair speechreader . . . . I believe there is a great future for it when its adaptability to various purposes becomes better understood.

In conclusion she stated,

Speechreading is essentially an intellectual excercise; the mechanical part performed by the eye . . . . is entirely subsidiary.

The aim of the speechreader should be to grasp a speaker's meaning as a complete whole, and not attempt to decipher it word by word or even sentence by sentence.

To those to whom the doors of sound are closed, the acquisition of the 'Subtile Art which may enable one with an observant Eie to Heare what any man speaks by the moving of his lips' is worth and well repays every possible effort to attain. (Deland, 1931, pp. 147-148)

Bell had been skeptical of the value of speechreading but came to uphold it strongly. Of his own methods of teaching the deaf Bell was

. . . one of the first to advocate that deaf children begin their learning of speech by imitation of whole words, with meaning. This was in opposition to the long-used element method, in which separate speech elements were taught first, then combined into meaningless syllables, before the child acquired speech words for communication. Under Bell's method, children were to be taught to understand whole words and sentences in lipreading and writing, and then to imitate the speech for them. Pronunciation was to be corrected as the child used the speech thus acquired. (Bender, 1960, pp. 159-160)

Alexander Graham Bell, with all of his varied contributions, has been unequaled in achieving worthwhile aid for the deaf. Through the strong feelings of Gallaudet and Bell an emerging combination of the oral and manual methods evolved. Oralism and manualism, a mixture of these two, and other innovations became the ages of controversy, remaining even today. Gallaudet felt that the convictions of both men should be aired to the public so a Washington Conference was held in 1868. All schools were represented. A resolution was passed that stated the following:

In the opinion of the Conference it is the duty of all institutions for the deaf and dumb to provide adequate means of imparting instruction in articulating and lipreading to such of their pupils as may be able to profit in exercises of this nature.

America accepted that diversity of methods which Bell later advocated to the Royal Commission, instead of the uniformity desired by so many European enthusiasts. It is this deversity, together with the wisdom which dictates that enough shall be spent instead of too little, which has made American education of the deaf the best in the world. (Hodgson, 1953, p. 283)

The advent of higher education for the deaf was another accomplishment during the nineteenth century. For this story the *Voice of the Deaf* by Maxine Tull Boatner (1959) gives the biography of Edward Miner Gallaudet (1837-1917).

Amos Kendall was unhappy with what he saw being done with young deaf children in Washington, D. C. and took it upon himself to change the picture. He offered his farm, then on the outskirts of the city, as a location for a school for the deaf and then began searching for a person to develop and run it. Learning of the Gallaudet influence, Kendall wrote to Hartford and although not anticipating such life work, Edward Miner Gallaudet accepted the challenge and went to Washington. The school began as a very small institution. Through the years Gallaudet was able to enlarge the physical facilities and the enrollment.

Soon after beginning his duties, Gallaudet developed his dream of a college for the deaf. He approached the proper authorities and was able to get a college established for the deaf by an act of Congress which was signed by Abraham Lincoln in 1864. The Columbia Institution for the Deaf became twofold. Kendall's school was the elementary and high school and Gallaudet College was the advanced school. Edward Miner Gallaudet became the first president and was responsibe for the realization of his dream. Established in 1865, Gallaudet College was named in honor of Thomas Hopkins Gallaudet and has been the world's only college for the deaf for these one hundred and four years.

The second president of the college was Percival Hall Sr. (1874-1954) and the third and present administrator is Leonard Elstad (1899-   ). The name of the institution is now Gallaudet College with Kendall School as the laboratory school for the college.

TWENTIETH CENTURY

Today the twentieth century is ours. How history will write these years remains to be seen. Certain observations, however, can be made of the age. Medicine has done remarkable research and has been able to combat some of the causes of deafness by drugs and by operations. The advent of amplification and the individual hearing aid are probably the greatest achievements of the time. Schools for the deaf, regardless of method, have been recognized as educational centers whether day or residential in nature. The public is aware of the handicapped and the deaf themselves are making integral contributions to society to mesh into the world at large as first class citizens.

Education for the deaf varies in its scope from nation to nation, but practically every part of the world has some mode of education for the deaf today. The problems of a fuller education continue to frustrate and challenge the profession. In conclusion these quotes from James Kerr Love in his book *The Deaf Child* (1911) seem appropriate.

> Many teachers . . . are so full of their method that they cannot see the deaf child for their method. Teachers have divided themselves into opposing camps of oralists and manualists, and until this opposition ceases, the deaf child must suffer. (Love, 1911, p. 121)
>
> Why, in a single question, have teachers of the deaf divided themselves into two opposing camps for two or three hundred years, and why is there no real progress towards unanimity? Because the deaf have been, and still are, regarded as a homogeneous class, which they are not, they are brought together into large buildings and taught by a single method, when no one method can be successfully applied to them. (Love, 1911, p. 122)
>
> Forget the system, study the deaf child . . . . But the method must wait on the child, not the child on the method. The deaf child first, always the deaf child first. (Love, 1911, p. 123)
>
> Further progress in the education of the deaf-mute depends not on the study of methods of education, but on a study of the deaf themselves, a study which will give a scientific classification, and which will enable existing methods to be applied with greater efficiency. (Love, 1911, p. 124)

Chapter II

PRESCHOOL CONSIDERATIONS

THE YEARS BEFORE formal schooling begins are considered home-centered in their entirety. The parents dominate the scene and are responsible for the care, development and learning-growth of their children. There are guidelines that can help parents, and many resources are available. This chapter will deal as simply as possible with the needs of the preschool child; give helpful information to guide parents and list further resources.

The materials were prepared at the Iowa School for the Deaf in 1968 for the Conference of Executives of American Schools for the deaf.

EMOTIONAL ENVIRONMENT

A child's education begins at birth. He can be taught if his parents take time, have patience, and use methods within his grasp.

Each child is different and his interests vary. One need is the same for all. Acceptance of the child is basic to his happiness. Sincere love is a strong force in establishing security. The emotional climate does much to stimulate or hamper learning. His home environment has a real bearing on his future life. A warm and friendly home atmosphere should exist.

A child should be approached with calmness and understanding. Every child needs success; he needs to know that his parents recognize his efforts.

It is important that parents be consistent from day to day and support each other. Training requires direction in a simple, clear manner. A child likes routine and benefits from a regular schedule of eating, sleeping, toileting, and playing. Children's attitudes toward these aspects of their life are influenced by their early training.

A child should be given responsibility within his scope of performance. This will help him mature. As he develops, he should be taught to look after his own personal wants. All members of the family need to share in the duties and benefits of the household. It is important that children be informed of happenings in their families, even if it has to be through pictures or snapshots. The deaf child is the same as anyone else, for he wants to be included in activities. This gives him a sense of belonging.

If overprotection and overindulgence exist, they deprive the child of growth toward independence and self-confidence. His activties should be similar to those of the hearing child but suited to his age and ability.

Avoid indifference and rejection. Such behavior lessens a child's security and causes him to feel neither loved nor valued.

Every child must learn that part of living requires abiding within certain lines of authority. In the beginning he has no respect for rights. Through teaching, he learns to comply harmoniously with others. Wise and effective judgment on the part of his parents help a child act properly in his environment. Corrective measures can be successful in a logical, unexcitable, and symapthetic manner. Ignoring behavior standards because a child is deaf is not fair to him or to his brothers and sisters. It may take longer to explain these standards, but they can be understood.

Discipline of the deaf need not differ from that of the hearing child. If he exhibits misconduct, his parents should look for clues as they would in other children of the same age. He must comprehend the grounds for his parents' reaction. Generally the most meaningful approach is a firm and consistent policy related to the present time.

Excessive temper tantrums, quarreling, and stubbornness signify all is not well with a child. Try and find out what is causing this behavior. Sometimes the lack of verbal expression or inability to interpret fully a given situation accurately may frustrate him.

PHYSICAL ENVIRONMENT

It is wise to arrange home and equipment so the child can

manage for himself. He should be permitted to do a task whenever he is capable. If time is taken to show him how to use materials and equipment carefully, he will be able to accomplish a great deal. A process should be broken down into small distinct steps to be taught.

Remember, children develop at unlike rates. Achievements reflect not only the child's abilities, but also his environmental influences. Concern is not warranted unless marked deviation exists, then a pediatrician should be contacted.

Landmark Skills

Landmark skills are noticeable during the growth process. These milestones parellel various ones on the Vineland Social Maturity Scale by Edgar A. Doll, Ph. D.

Before the First Birthday

1. Lifts a cup or glass and drinks out of it with assistance.

2. Holds head and back stable.

3. Moves about on the floor by crawling or creeping.

4. Pulls himself up to a standing position.
5. Stands on a firm surface.

Before the Second Birthday

6. Walks independently.
7. Scribbles with a pencil.
8. Drinks from a cup.

9 .Uses a spoon to eat from a cup or bowl.
10. Climbs upstairs without the help of someone.
11. Picks up and carries things.

Before the Third Birthday

12. Puts on and removes his coat or dress.
13. Eats with a fork.

14. Dries hands if washed.
15. Makes known a desire to go to the toilet.

Before the Fourth Birthday

16. Puts on and buttons coat or dress.
17. Washes hands.

18. Cooperates with sharing and taking turns.
19. Does short errands and little household duties.

Before the Fifth Birthday

20. Does ordinary dressing with the exception of tying ribbons, laces or ties. Could have help with the difficult or close-fitting clothes.

21. Washes own face.
22. Makes a simple drawing.

23. Goes to the toilet alone and has overcome daytime "accidents."

24. Plays in a small group of children of the same age, such games as tag, hide-and-seek, etc.

HOME TRAINING

All too frequently parents of young deaf children are over-whelmed by the idea of assuming the role of teacher in addition to the many other important affairs of their busy lives. Teaching in our age implies a structured academic setting with predeter-mined objectives and special methods for reaching these goals. Parents are not expected to institute a formal classroom. For-tunately, the home is a rich laboratory for learning. There is a wealth of material in the child's natural surroundings which pro-vides an excellent atmosphere for him.

Relaxation is of primary importance. Tenseness and anxiety hamper communications between the parent and child; uneasi-ness prevents parents from giving fully of themselves. Parents, as the primary model, must be worthy of their child's respect. This will be gained through effective discipline, the prerequisite to all watching, listening, and learning. A warm personality and steadfast perseverance are also vital requirements.

Discovering a hearing problem while the child is still very young is important. Even after the parents have found that their child is deaf, they should talk, talk, and talk some more to him. They should speak to him naturally, at a moderate rate, not exaggerating or shouting, but as they would speak to a hearing child.

His attention will be heightened if he is looking at a happy face full of expression and affection. Parents should accept every bit of achievement with joy, regardless of how slow it may seem. They should not expect immediate speech. If the child happens to say a particular word or phrase, be pleased and do not have him continue with so many repetitions that he becomes bored and perhaps refuses further verbalizations.

Parents should look at pictures with him and point out details (see Fig. 1). In choosing a book pick one with a few words on a page and in the range of the child's experience and appeal. It is enjoyable for him to act out the story and its vocabulary.

FIGURE 1

In working with the child there are several things to take into account such as age, interests, and hand coordination. The very young child delights in holding and manipulating objects; therefore, the matching of large, identical things seems to be a reasonable starting point. The order that should be followed is one that best suits the parents and their child. Success depends upon the parents recognition of his individuality and proficiency rather than upon some set pattern.

Associating objects with pictures helps the child to visualize the connection between the pictorial items and the real ones. A number of objects can be repeated in many different ways by making them more complicated as insight develops (see Fig. 2).

FIGURE 2

Then, on a higher level, pictures may be matched (see Fig. 3). These are only a few illustrations. By using imagination any number of materials accessible at home can be used to incorporate and improve skills in addition to providing fun for the child.

For a child who must acquire language through sight, vibration, and the little hearing he has left (residual hearing), it is of prime importance that he be motivated to listen in order

FIGURE 3

to become cognizant of sound. When there is a loud noise, let him know you heard something. Show him the source of the loud noise or give him a picture of what made it. The child should have a chance to be exposed to sounds of the telephone, doorbell, running water, corn popping, washing machine, vacuum cleaner, lawn mower, animals, and the alarm clock. Awareness and recognition of the fire siren, car horn, etc., are crucial for safety purposes.

Nature can be enjoyed more if the child is directed toward the sound of the birds chirping, the rustle of leaves when the wind is blowing or the crunching of snow to mention only some.

Music has charm even for the small deaf boy or girl. Parents should sing to him while he is sitting on their laps. Even though little hearing exists he will feel the vibrations from their bodies. The child should become acquainted with loud and soft music. By placing his hands on the piano or the record player he will notice the music and discriminate between the presence or absence of sound.

HEARING LOSS AND HEARING AIDS

If there is a question about the child's hearing, see an ear physician—an otologist or otolaryngologist—for a careful and thorough medical examination in order to investigate whether there is any abnormality in the hearing mechanism and to evaluate the child's background for any past conditions which might have affected hearing. He will be able to determine if the child can be helped by surgery, by medicine, by hearing aid or by training. For the name of a specialist the family physician, local medical society, or the yellow pages of the telephone directory may be consulted. The diagnosis from a reputable ear doctor or medical clinic will generally suffice. Traveling from one expert to another usually results in similar recommendations.

Before purchasing the hearing aid, it is wise for parents to go to a hearing evaluation center, where audiologists will counsel them in an appropriate selection. Parents can visit a hearing and speech clinic in a university or a nearby city. The state school for the deaf serves as a source of information on this matter also.

If in doubt in regard to any hearing aid dealer, check the Better Business Bureau. Many dealers will lend or rent an aid on a trial basis for performance observation. Parents should be on guard against signing a contract to purchase a unit while negotiating a rental agreement. In choosing an aid it is advantageous to consider availability and cost of repair as well as quality of product.

The audiologist who measures the child's hearing on an audiometer will be able to discuss his results with the parents. The composite findings are plotted graphically on an audiogram.

Only presumptive evidence may be available in determining the actual degree of hearing with the very young tot. Methods for ascertaining the true level of hearing are more suitable to those above four years. Not only one, but periodic evaluations are commonly given.

As soon as an impairment is diagnosed, an attempt may be made to try amplified sound in order to stimulate vocalization and natural babbling. Maturity and personality are factors to consider rather than chronological age alone. Force is not recommended.

Although the child may not perceive speech and language

with his aid, he will profit even if he discerns only the very loud environmental sounds such as doorbells, car horns, and fire alarms.

Before he ever wears his aid, build an interest by talking about it and showing him pictures. Try to make the first day an important occasion in his life. In the beginning see that his experiences are pleasant and gradual.

Parents will have to supervise the care and upkeep of the aid until the child learns to assume the responsibility. The more he knows about his aid the greater concern he shows in relation to it.

Most hearing aid companies have a carrier to be worn either on the front or under outer clothing. This vest-like garment will hold the aid in place and not allow it to come loose or drop from position.

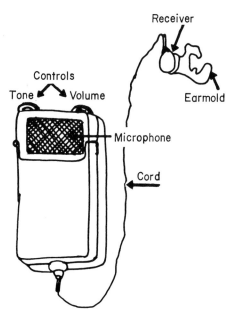

Often an eighteen-inch cord is advisable. An extra cord should be kept on hand in case of need. "Cut-outs" may be checked by rolling the cord gently back and forth between your fingers as you hold the receiver to your ear. Chewing and twisting may cause a short in the cord.

For some very small children parents should put the ear-mold and receiver to their own ear, slightly turn the volume control and listen before they give the child the aid. The switch should be turned to *off* before inserting or removing the earmold.

After a period of time, worn controls may produce inter-mittent sound. Accumulated dust in this region can bring about scratchiness. A yearly check and cleaning by a factory hearing aid service representative would be advantageous.

The battery operates as the supplier of power and is con-nected with the sound system. The markings on the aid and on the batteries indicate how to proceed. If no sound is audible, fresh batteries should be installed or the cord changed. Weak batteries may cause poor auditory reception, therefore the bat-teries should be taken from the hearing aid when not in use, such as bedtime. Batteries should be kept in a cool, dry place. Dampness may lead to corrosion.

A corroded battery terminal connection can be cleaned with a pencil eraser or scraped with a knife. A scratchy or hiss-ing noice may result if corroding parts are neglected.

A bit of petroleum jelly placed on the exterior of a tight-fitting earmold will ease its insertion. As a child grows, ears change slightly in size and shape. A new custom earmold may be necessary. The new earmold should not be too loose, for whistling may occur or sound may leak from around the earmold into the microphone. The greater the distance between the micro-phone and the receiver, the less chance of feedback. Feedback may also indicate that the child put his aid at full volume.

The mold may be cleaned with soap and warm water or a specially prepared type of cleaner but not alocohol. The canal section may be cleaned with a pipe cleaner.

Wax may block sound or cause feedback. It is beneficial to have the child's ears checked by an ear specialist at least once a year.

PROFESSIONAL HELP AND INFORMATION

A preschool program designed especially for the deaf is helpful. If this is not available, the parents should attempt to find a teacher of the deaf or a speech and hearing clinic to assist them with at least one lesson a week. This individual or agency can give ideas on what to do in the home.

The local superintendent or State Department of Education may advise the parents on facilities available for the deaf and hard of hearing. Many colleges and universities have hearing clinics which offer a similar service.

The Alexander Graham Bell Association for the Deaf, Inc., 1537-35th Street, N. W., Washington, D. C. 20007, fosters the teaching of speech and lipreading to the deaf. It has established the International Parents' Organization for those searching for a better understanding of the hearing impaired child. Headquarters of the Association, The Volta Bureau, serves as an information center, gives replies through correspondence, and operates one of the largest library collections on deafness in the world. Membership in the group entitles parents to the use of the lending library and a subscription to the official journal, *The Volta Review*. A list of its publications available for purchase will be sent upon request.

The American Hearing Society, 919 - 18th Street, N.W., Washington, D. C. 20006, distributes many helps for parents of hearing impaired children. This organization promotes early identification and prevention of deafness, conservation of hearing, rehabilitation measures with the acoustically impaired, speech instruction, auditory training, speech reading classes and hearing aid counseling.

The American Medical Association, 535 North Dearborn Street, Chicago, Illinois 60610, can be contacted in reference to hearing problems.

The American Speech and Hearing Association, 9030 Old Georgetown Road, Washington, D. C. 20014, which is a group whose members are educated to give services in speech and hearing, has a record of qualified persons certified according to the Association's requirements.

The Conference of Executives of American Schools for the Deaf and the Convention of American Instructors of the Deaf, Gallaudet College, Washington, D. C. 20002, the organizations for administrators and teachers, will disseminate information to parents and schools and will answer specific questions. These bodies act jointly to encourage high standards and professional growth for educating the deaf in America.

The Council for Exceptional Children, 1201 - 16th Street, N. W., Washington, D. C. 20036, a department of the National Education Association, strives to advance educational opportunities for all kinds of exceptional youngsters. It has chapters in many states and cities.

The John Tracy Clinic, 806 West Adams Boulevard, Los Angeles, California 90007, offers a correspondence course of twelve monthly installments for parents of preschool children, free upon request.

The National Society for Crippled Children and Adults, Inc., 2023 West Ogden Avenue, Chicago, Illinois 60612, which has a number of local societies, is concerned about many handicaps including the deaf and hard of hearing. This group will mail information to parents. The Easter Seal Research Foundation comes under its jurisdiction.

Hearing aid manufacturers send out much literature upon request. When a particular area of interest is indicated, the material may be more worthwhile. The following are names of hearing aid manufacturers offering free information.

Beltone Electronics Corporation
4201 West Victoria Street
Chicago, Illinois 60646

Maico Electronics
7375 Bush Lake Road
Minneapolis, Minnesota 55435

Radioear Corporation
Valley Brook Road
Canonsburg, Pennsylvania 15317

Sonotone Corporation
Elmsford, New York 10523

Vicon Instrument Company
Colorado Springs, Colorado 80901

Zenith Hearing Aid Sales Corporation

6501 West Grand Avenue
Chicago, Illinois 60635

Materials in various media are available to parents and teachers alike. A bibliography of available materials follows.

Books

Ewing, Irene R., and Alexander, W. G.: *New Opportunities for Deaf Children.* Springfield, Thomas, 1960.

Harris, Grace M.: *Language for the Preschool Deaf Child.* New York, Grune, 1963.

Myklebust, Helmer R.: *Your Deaf Child: A Guide for Parents.* Springfield, Thomas, 1960.

Utley, Jean: *What's It's Name?* Urbana, Ill., U. of Ill., 1950.

Utley, Jean: *Auditory Training Album.* Urbana, Ill., U. of Ill., 1950.

Pamphlets

Harris, Grace M.: *For Parents of Very Young Deaf Children.**

Pollack, Dorren C. and Marion P. Downs: *A Parent's Guide to Hearing Aids for Young Children.**

Robinson, Geoffrey C., M. D. et al.: *Pediatrics and Disorders in Communication.*

Van Wyk, Mark K.: *Beginning Speechreading.**

Volta Bureau: *List of Schools and Classes for Deaf Children Under Six in Canada.**

*List of Schools and Classes for Deaf Children Under Six in U. S. A.**

Keaster, Jacqueline, and Gloria Hoversten: *Suggestions to the Parents of Pre-School Children with Hearing Impairment.* The American Academy of Ophthalmology and Otolaryngology, 15 Second Street, S. W., Rochester, Minn. 55901

*All pamphlets marked with an asterisk and all books may be purchased from the Alexander Graham Bell Association for the Deaf, Inc., 1537 Thirty-Fifth Street, N. W., Washington, D. C. 20007.

Films

A New Life for Jennifer. (16 mm color-sound production of 27 minutes. Free rental, Lutheran School for the Deaf, 6861 East Nevada Avenue, Detroit, Michigan 48234)

Depicts a four year old deaf child being taught in school. It received the 1965 Blue Ribbon Award at the American Flm Festival in New York City.

Silent World-Muffled World. 16mm color-sound film, 28 minutes in length. Free rental or purchase for $100. U. S. Public Health Service. Audiovisual Facility, Atlanta, Georgia 30333.

This documentary narrated by Gregory Peck portrays actual classroom scenes, the problems of deafness, a surgical operation on the middle ear and suggests future developments in medical research into deafness.

Chapter III

EDUCATING YOUTH

THE AMERICAN PUBLIC SCHOOL

T HE SCHOOL YEARS occupy about thirteen years in the lives of young people. For those who continue their education into college and/or post-school programs these years of concentrated learning are extended. The attention of everyone focuses on education with great vigor. Many people are extremely opinionated when they discuss the nation's educational system. It would seem that the sudden accomplishment by Russia with "Sputnik" in 1957, putting the United States in the space age, immediately condemned its present schools and made every citizen of the nation an expert on how schools should function. The general tone of the citizenry's advice has been negative criticism and very often it is given without any investigation or background of the situation. (Negative and positive criticism given after thoughtful consideration is a valuable asset to any school). The criticisms usually rendered are pointed at the administrators, school boards, or teachers. However, the main character in any school is the student. It is the student who makes education necessary at all. Therefore, education is a two-way street. All schools are trying to work with all students and this is the changing concept of which most critics of schools are not aware.

In the past decades only those children who had the ability to learn easily went to school for any length of time. The poor students (but not necessarily of low intelligence), the educationally retarded, the borderline low intelligence, the mentally retarded, and certain other types, went to school only a few years or were not admitted at all. Drop-out notes to go to work were high. Working often caused irregular attendance for some and these often dropped out in due time. With this situation the good student with ability proceeded rapidly and was a good or above-average scholar.

Recognizing that this was not an ideal situation, lawmakers for various reasons established age limits for children to go to school and all students were encouraged to remain in school. This change in educational policy and procedure threw most of the schools out of balance and created many problems that could not immediately be solved satisfactorily. *The basic philosophy of schools had changed from one of educating only the able to one of educating all that enter.* Once this basic difference is recognized, school appraisal must also be done in a more realistic light.

Today *all types* of children are in our schools. Our task is to give some type of education to all of them which is commensurate with their abilities. In schools for the deaf, as well as all public schools, the goal is the same. That is, *to put into society a human being who is able to contribute as well as to enjoy all that our civilization has to offer, regardless of handicap, mental ability, or any other shortcoming a person might have.*

Educators and Students

It takes a special type of person to work in this educational situation, whether as an administrator or teacher. A person must have confidence, the ability to understand children, and the ability to inspire the student to put forth his finest efforts, and professional training. The teacher or administrator is only one side of the school situation, however, and the adult in command cannot do the job alone. The student has a responsibility also. The student must be ready, willing, and able to accept what the school offers. Once the student understands his role in education, the task becomes easier for everyone.

Teachers

1. Accept all the pupils that enter the classrooms for what they are. Those that can excel should be urged to aspire for college and specialized training. All available resources should be channeled into making these students understand what higher education can do for them. Students not so gifted must reach their peaks of ability and broaden their understanding horizontally.

2. Teachers must be firm, fair, and friendly with *all* students.

3. Teachers must recognize the limits of the multiple handicapped and try to find where they can excel.

4. Instructing slower students should not make teachers feel discriminated against. These students are a special challenge and their education is as vital to society as education of the brighter students.

5. Remember, teaching is possibly the most important profession of all as they mold the citizens of tomorrow.

Students

1. Take advantage of available opportunities.

2. Do not be afraid to work hard to fulfill school assignments. Even though days are full of activity, extra time can be given to study if time is used efficiently.

3. Students should be respectful and courteous to teachers, counsellors, administrators—*all adults*. Adjusting harmoniously to one seniors is vital in this business of living.

4. Students must learn to live with their peers, too. Courtesy and respect are essential to intra-group relationships. Everyone is different and everyone has something to contribute to living and learning.

5. Students should cooperate with school officials to attain the best possible education.

Education does not come easily. When both the educational staff and the students work together, the end result is gratifying. The schools are then able to give society the people it needs for its own perpetuation—physicians, dentists, scientists, teachers, journalists, political leaders, artists, technicians, skilled craftsmen, unskilled workers, and everyone else who keep this world going. With this knowledge perhaps the citizenry can give our educational system the understanding, patience, and helpful criticism it needs—and perhaps even an occasional pat on the back.

Education Principles

The National Education Association established seven cardinal principles for education in 1918 that have been a guide to schools ever since. Keeping these seven goals in mind administrators and teachers are better able to judge their work and determine the success or failure of programs used in schools. These seven principles are health, command of fundamental processes, vocation, worthy home membership, citizenship, worthy use of leisure time and ethical character.

Social and personal efficiency depend upon health. Schools can teach certain facts about health, help students form good health habits and build proper attitudes toward health. Emphasis on health should be a continuous process crossing all lines of instruction and activities within a school—not just a semester course taught now and then within the curriculum.

Command of fundametal processes generally refers to basic skills of reading, writing, and artihmetic. These are learned at different rates by students so that proficiency is achieved at various levels. Exercises should continually stress these fundamentals so that proficiency is maintained and/or deficiencies discovered for remedial work. Skills should continually increase through the school years. Too often school personnel become so involved with this area of education that other vitally important areas are overlooked or at least greatly diminished in their importance.

Vocational efficiency is a social aim for most everyone at some time in life, as almost everyone is responsible for his own, and probably others', welfare. The schools are aware of this need and have placed more emphasis on vocational needs. The multitude of different occupations, periods of training required and changing society requires adaptation of vocation goals. There is a demand for graduates with some degree of skills. Schools must be careful not to overemphasize vocational work, as other aims should not be neglected. Stress should be on all the principles as they relate to each other. In high schools, high proficiency in a given vocational task is not attainable or desirable, however, there is time for students to explore types of training and aptitudes as they become acquainted with the world of work. These experiences enable students to make a wise choice of their own vocation.

Citizenship is another principle that can best be taught indirectly. Saluting the flag, repeating the oath of allegiance, or studying the constitution will not produce true loyalty. Activities and experience must make these symbolic activities develop meaning. All school subjects and activities help foster good citizenship. Ultimately, a person should develop so as to become a wholesome member of his community, state, nation and the world. Therefore, a person must develop many side interests to benefit his welfare and that of others, He must also attain a sense of civic righteousness in his cooperation with others in social action.

Worthy use of leisure time becomes a more and more important goal of education, as the work day becomes shorter and household chores are lessened by automation. Leisure activities should be recreational, healthful and perhaps educational. Schools should teach students how to use the resources available in their homes and communities as rewarding leisure pursuits. School activities can cultivate this idea in the selection of activities it provides.

Crime and delinquency have revealed that youth who are incapable of directing their own conducts are a menace to society. Therefore, every effort should be made by schools to develop good ethical character in students. Again, this aim probably can be best taught indirectly and by example. The total school program contributes to ethical character. For example, good sportsmanship in sports, honesty in school work, respect for property, and respect for rules and authority are desirable characteritics that lead to strong wholesome characters in students.

It is necessary to understand the importance of the home as a social institution and find one's place and duties within the framework of the home. Although teaching home membership should be done incidentally, the outcome of the teaching is of prime importance. School is not home and it would not be desirable for it to be so. There can be a transfer of learning from one to the other, however. There are common elements in both and being a worthy member of one situation can carry over into the other. Further, observation by the students of adult staff members in their home relationships teaches more than is apparent many times.

It would be impossible to discuss in detail the many facets of education today. However, observations in some areas of thought are possible.

INSTRUCTION OF THE DEAF

The Iowa School for the Deaf, Council Bluffs, has been the source of understanding for much of the material presented and some in this chapter is taken from articles previously written by the authors.

The following reprint of an editorial in the *Iowa Hawkeye*, January 1966, summarizes the place of the residential school in society today.

THE IOWA SCHOOL OFFERS A COMPLETE PROGRAM

This past fall there were inquiries from a few parents as to our feelings in regard to two small day classes which have been opened in isolated parts of the state. It caused some parents moments of anxiety and caused much soul searching. Parents had to weigh the pros and cons of the one room school vs. the residential school. The one room school does keep the child close to home but there are many arguments concerning this type of program. No attempt will be made to list them here. Instead, here is what the residential school has to offer and then parents can easily see why there is a need for the residential type facility:

1. The Iowa School for the Deaf has a goal - to give its students the best education they are capable of achieving. Its curriculum is well balanced with a beginning and an end. It is well graded and in most instances tries to fit the curriculum to the child. In addition to academic learning the Iowa School for the Deaf offers excellent vocational training, training in social living, stresses good moral and ethical standards and emphasizes understanding of the responsibility of citizenship. These goals are met because of the very nature of the organization of the school: (a) size (b) personnel (c) curriculum (d) special services.

2. Students at the Iowa School for the Deaf are respected and treated the same as children in any good school. While students, they take part and benefit from the same social and recreational activities as their peers in public schools. For example, our students are in an athletic conference which competes against area high high schools in football, basketball, track and wrestling. In this healthy competition the students show that they can compete successfully and that they can excel.

3. Further training in the role of living is given through extra-curricular activities. The Iowa School for the Deaf is proud of its record in the field. Led by the volunteer efforts of teachers and dormitory personnel, this program includes Scouting, Sub-Teens, Homemakers' Club, Pixies, "I" Club, Trap Shooting Club, Pep Club, Class organizations, Year Book, Mardi Gras, Red Cross, Hobby Club and Y-Teens. In many of these organizations the boys and girls are constantly mixing with children in the community and learning to get along with them.

4. The Iowa School for the Deaf offers special services including audiology, psychology and vocational guidance to all its students.

In short, the Iowa School blends its educational and vocational program with personal and social development which give the child a well-balanced program. The final product of these efforts is an educated, happy, well-adjusted adult ready for advanced training, college or work. The success of this program is proven by the excellent progress which Iowa School for the Deaf graduates are making in industry, business, education and other fields. There is a constant demand for our students in many industries.

The one room school does not and cannot offer a similarly well-rounded program. Throughout our nation the trend in education is toward well organized consolidated school units and away from the one room country school. A residential school for the deaf is this type of consolidated school. To go to one room classes for the deaf seems a step backwards. Further, if the people who are constantly pushing one room programs would seriously consider the effects of deafness they would learn to understand that students so handicapped require a special approach to education. Education of the hearing impaired belongs in the hands of specially trained personnel working in a well-coordinated program if optimum results are to be attained. The Iowa School for the Deaf meets these standards and is continually striving to improve upon its service of excellence to the hearing impaired and the State of Iowa.

SCHOOL CURRICULUM AREAS

Hearing, Speech and Speechreading

When the general public hears or thinks of a school for the deaf, the immediate impression is that all the students are deaf. That is, they think that none of the students have any hearing. The name, SCHOOL OF THE DEAF, reinforces this implication. This misunderstanding is causing much difficulty, both inside and beyond the school.

The fact is that a great majority of the students in a school for the deaf have some residual hearing. Very, very few of them are deaf. Therefore, one of the greatest tasks facing educators of the deaf is that of developing whatever hearing is available, so that it may be utilized in the education of the child with impaired hearing.

The importance of hearing in education can be appreciated by realizing that a student in a regular public school spends from one-half to two-thirds of the day in listening. He listens to instructions, to class discussions, to conversation, to reports, to reading, to teacher comments, to outside noises, etc. He is learning and gaining much information by listening.

The child with impaired hearing misses most of this listening approach to learning. By the proper use of auditory training, however, the child with a hearing loss can benefit from the spoken word. This can be a very strong supplement to whatever other methods of educational instruction are employed.

Many schools for the deaf are equipped with the latest electronic equipment available for hearing amplification. Gallaudet College has opened what is probably the most modern hearing and speech center in the world. Many universities and electronic companies are working hard through research to develop better and improved hearing aid equipment. There seems to be a healthy trend all over the nation to help those with impaired hearing. In too many schools, however, auditory equipment is not fully utilized. After pupils leave Primary Departments, much equipment lies idle and the use of hearing is not fully employed. This wastes valuable talent and ignores an avenue of learning as well.

Dr. Leonard Elstad, President of Gallaudet College, told the Gallaudet College student body to take full advantage of the training provided for them by the speech and hearing center. Dr. Elstad said, "The use of the language of signs at the college does not mean that a student cannot have good speech too. You are going to live with hearing people and compete in a business world made up mainly of hearing people. Even those of you with very poor speech can benefit by training in the center. *If you have a remnant of hearing, learn to use it. Make use of your potential.*"

There is little more to add to Dr. Elstad's remarks. Hearing and speech are important. It is the duty of all educators to encourage deaf students to use whatever method of instruction is employed. No effort in the area of speech and hearing should be relaxed at any time.

There is no reason why students in schools for the deaf across the nation can not make full use of whatever speech and hearing they may have. It will help them educationally, and in life after leaving school.

In evaluating speech it seems to culminate in one question. What should be the basis for the evaluation of speech? There is really only one answer, and that is whether or not the speech is understandable to the listener. The teacher should not be the sole listener. The listener is any person the child comes in contact with in any place.

In speech there is a problem of how to report progress or give grades. Probably the best type of report is a written report by the teacher rather than a single grade. It is very difficult to interpret a single grade effectively. When a teacher writes what is being done in the classroom the parent is better able to compare and contrast the written remarks with his personal observations of the child. The parent says, "I can't understand my child." The teacher writes that the child's speech is not intelligible at the present time but various activities are taking place at school which should improve the situation in the future. This type of rapport makes it possible for both the parent and the school to work together without being defeated by a negative failing attitude which a single grade of "D" or "F" might have created. Ultimately, both the home and school want intelligible, understandable speech and the wholesome environment for this achievement must be optimum in both places for the best possible results. Only a positive and encouraging approach can succeed.

Speechreading ability seems to require a particular type of mind. The mind must be receptive, relaxed and synthetic in nature for the ultimate in understanding. A rather good comparison is speechreading and piano playing. Most anyone can learn something of the ability to play the piano. Many can reach a point of ability that playing the piano for self, family or friends is enjoyable. Some can play confidently in public places such as in churches and for community affairs, but the number of virtuosos is select. The same is true of speechreading.

The past several years have been interesting ones for comparison in techniques, methods and abilities in speechreading in teacher training classes of upper class undergraduate and graduate students from the University of Omaha and the University of Iowa. As a requirement the students have had to teach their fellow students one period during the term. It was clearly understood that class grades would be given on teaching technique but not on speechreading ability. In the initial years certain requirements were enforced and the students taught, in order, according to the visibility of certain letters (p, b, m lessons first as the most visible, to k, the least visible). The lessons were to begin simply and progress to the more difficult with serious consultation of Nitchie, Kinzie, and Mueller Walle books. These early classes succeeded, but not with enthusiastic results. There seemed a degree of unidentifiable boredom and resigned lack even though the restrictions set up left plenty of room for individual ideas and creativity. Of course, many variables were always present. The course is never really the same any two years, but the idea of being a teacher and student seemed sound enough to be incorporated each time the course has been given.

After four years of being dissatisfied with the results, a hunch to try something different was realized. In some private tutoring being done success was in the relationship with the student and teacher, not the procedure of following a specific pattern of any of the methods that have been established as good—Nitchie, Mueller Walle, Kinzie, Jena.

The crux of the matter seemed to be the following points:

1. Not only knowing, but *understanding* the person being worked with.

2. Developing a rapport that was really a friendship with the student.

3. Because of the above the teacher-student time together was something *both* looked forward to.

4. *Both* had things(objects or ideas) *to share* with the other.

5. Because circumstances were so congenial and relaxed and fun the object of being together was soon unthought of as a learning period per se but almost pure Pestalozzian— learning because we wanted to learn. There was no easy-to-harder approach or letter to syllable to word to phrase to sentence work. Simply stated, the teacher and student shared ideas. "Grasping wholes" as Comenius (1592-1671) points out "comes before parts."

6. The physical basis was automatic—good lighting, position in relationship with the student, etc.

With this innovation the teacher training class was no longer assigned letter positions or given guidelines. The results were gratifying. Given some basic background and suggestions the students can do anything they want. The class has a reputation—everyone wants to take it. No one wants to be absent because the things which happen are too good to miss. The fun is unsurpassed, the creativity superb, and the learning that takes place, amazing. The speechreading ability of the students is unbelievable.

Find yourself, be yourself and express yourself, and do likewise with your students. Combine physical techniques and Pestalozzian philosophy, and speechreading results will be gratifying.

English

English at any level should be based on creativity. First-hand experiences of the child and material that is relevant to the real life of the student should be the prime criteria for work. Learning to write effectively with communication is always an obvious goal. However, there must be plenty of time for conversation in a group. Speech as an expression of English is usually not given its proper place and should be utilized to better advantage. Student envolvement is essential. Drama is also an effective medium at all levels and should not be overlooked. Literature and enrichment are sufficient goals unto themselves. Expression in all its forms must grace the classroom experience for students to feel stimulated to action and lifelong learning.

Elementary

Hearing children learn language before they start going to school. They have an understanding of language long before they are able to talk. They hear language constantly from the time they are born; it just comes naturally as a part of growing. They see a situation and hear the language and sounds which accompany that situation. They hear others talk and gradually acquire words and expressions for their own use.

Children with hearing losses are deprived of the opportunity to learn language in this manner. They see the situations

at hand, but they do not hear the language or sound that accompanies it. Because of this they do not learn language on the same plan as the hearing child. As a direct consequence, they enter school equipped with no language or with language abilities below that of normal hearing children.

The basic problem, therefore, is finding an effective method of teaching language. How to do this is a problem familiar to all who have worked with children with hearing problems. From experiences in the classroom, the *news* or *sharing* period is one the most effective means of language instruction. The writing of daily news is an informal approach to language that can be made both interesting and meaningful. Good planning by the teacher can add color and lustre to this daily event. If properly handled, children will look forward to the opportunity of telling the class their thoughts and experiences. It is most important to make this period lively to attain maximum results. This factor lies primarily in the hands of the teacher.

A question heard many times is, "How can children who live in an institution tell something different every day?" Through experience it *is* possible. It only needs expert guidance by the teacher. It is necessary to make the child aware of his environment and curious about all the little things going on around him. A red letter event isn't the only thing that can make news fascinating. Children can become intensely interested in commonplace events or little aspects of nature which might ordinarily be unnoticed.

Here are some of the techniques which have been used and some examples of the daily news developed through the year. The class was a second preparatory class in the Kendall School. Gallaudet College, Washington, D. C. All but one of the pupils started in a preschool and had two years of formal training.

The *news* period was held the first thing in the morning while the children were fresh, beginning with a general discussion of any topic. To stimluate language a teacher could use a newspaper, magazine, pictures, or various objects. In the discussion that followed it was often necessary to use pictures and diagrams to help make the class more meaningful. Short sentences were used in descriptions and new words carefully explained. Sometimes the teacher told a class what was heard on the radio. Examples of discussions include such topics as baseball, current news, and the weather. There were lively discussions about the Peurto Ricans shooting at the members of the House of Representatives, the H bomb tests and the activities of the President. A map was brought to the children's attention to explain trips taken by their teacher, family or friends. In fact, anything at all can come up in these discussions.

A daily weather report was a *must*. Not only did the children observe what the weather was at the moment but they were also interested in knowing what it would be in the future from what the teacher had heard on the radio or read in the paper. If the teacher forgot to volunteer this information the class promptly reminded him. The teacher also discussed plans with the class and events that took place at home. All of this interested the students very much. While talking to the children, new words and phrases were carefully explained. Before the news was erased from the board the new words were written on a chart for future reference and the chart was always in some conspicuous place in the room.

By the time the teacher stopped telling about events, the children were more than anxious to tell something that they had experienced. They took turns telling about what happened to them or what they had on their minds. This often entailed some of their plans for the future, their dreams and past events. They were made conscious of the fact that events were taking place all around them and that they should be very observant. With the proper attitude, the children did not miss a trick.

How long should a news period last? That depends entirely upon the situation. If an interesting event is taking place a teacher would be foolish to cut short a news period simply because the time allotted for the news period was up. On the other hand, it would be just as foolish to prolong a news period when actual news is exhausted. It is the amount of language provoking material that determines the amount of time to be taken up by a news period. Precise limits for this period cannot be set in advance.

In the beginning of the year news was written on the blackboard for the class. Once in a while a child wanted to come up and write a word. This was encouraged and as the year progressed the children participated more and more until they were able to write practically all of their own news. After all the news

was on the blackboard, the children copied it into notebooks
reserved for that purpose.

Here is an example of the news written by the pupils.

September 28

NEWS

Louis has a Supermouse mask.
Bobby has a little brown comb.
Martha rode her bike yesterday.
Brad has two gold fish at home.
We all went to church yesterday.

As the children copied the news, the teacher had an opportunity to do individual speech work. All the written work was
carefully checked to correct any mistakes which might have
been made. The children's spoken and written vocabulary increased rapidly. They were then able to write their own sentences. Only new words were written on the board by the
teacher. These were then inserted where needed by the children. As the year progressed the news became longer and more
interesting. Here is another example of written news:

October 10

NEWS

A little boy *scratched* Bobby this morning.
He did not *hurt* him.
Martha *went* to church with her mother yesterday.
Brad *has* some candy cigarettes upstairs.
His mother *gave* them to him.
Mr. Giangreco *went* on a picnic yesterday. He *had* fun.

At this point straight copy work was stopped and the verbs
were taken out of the news. The underlined words were erased
from context and listed out of order on another part of the
board. Thus, the children were required to pick out the correct
word for each sentence.

This type of exercise helped the child understand that a
sentence is a meaningful unit. It helped to promote the ability
to use context clues and it was also a check on the identification
of word forms.

The news began to take on new meaning and form as time

went on. There was some repetition of the old material and a continuous increase in new material. As the news became longer, more complicated expressions were used. A greater number of words were taken out for the recopy exercise. This further emphasized the fact that the sentence is a meaningful unit.

Additional examples of the children's follow:

January 10

NEWS

Louis' father *came* to a P.T.A. meeting last *night*.
Louis *did not see* him.
Brad's mother *came* to school *last night*. She *went* to the *dormitory* to see *Brad*. He *was* very happy.
Louis *can* ride his *bike* alone now. He *is* happy.
Bobby, Brad, Louis and Byron played *basketball* yesterday. They *had* fun.
Martha *watched* television last night. She saw *Superman*. He was *good*.
Louis and Byron *will go* to Cub *Scouts* tonight.
We will all go *swimming* Thursday *afternoon*.

Again words were just taken out at random. By this time the children had mastered the spelling of common words well enough that only new words needed to be put on the board. They knew the old words and how to use them in a sentence. The class did very well in this respect, in spite of the difficulty of such a plan.

Paragraphing was begun at this point. The children were given a simple explanation of the paragraph. They were shown that sentences about the same subject were put in one group. Sentences about another subject were put in a different group.

March 18

NEWS

Macon *is* our cub *scout leader*. He is a boy *scout,* too.
Martha *went* to the *snack bar* yesterday. She *bought* some candy. It *cost* five *cents*.
We *played* on the *jungle gym* yesterday. It *was* fun.
Bobby *hurt* his *head* because he *was not* careful.
We will go *to the circus* next *Tuesday*. We *hope* it will be *good*.
Byron *dreamed* about *birds* last night.

Martha saw a *rcbin* and many *starlings* yesterday.
Bobby and Byron *played* tag yesterday *afternoon*.

The children were encouraged to write their own sentences without any help from the teacher. One child wrote the following in addition to the group news:

Bobby is a very bad boy.
Miss Walker gave us five new books yesterday.
We told her, "Thank you."
We will all go home tomorrow.
Mrs. Von gave us some candy last night.
Louis and I will see *Topper* on T.V. tomorrow.

The children were now thinking and writing sentences on their own. When anything came up they tried to write about it. With the teacher's help it was corrected, and the child learned the correct language.

The following conclusions are about the effectiveness of *news* as a means of developing straight language.

1. A good news period gives the child an opportunity to see correctly written language.

2. The child has an opportunity to write correct language.

3. It gives the child an opportunity to express his own thoughts and feelings.

4. It gives the child an opportunity to use context clues as a check on the identification of word forms.

5. It helps strengthen the fact that a sentence is a meaningful unit.

6. It puts vocabulary in a child's working knowledge that would not be taught in any other part of the school activities.

7. It develops a vocabulary casually which helps in reading development.

8. It lays a good foundation for reading development.

9. It provides the opportunity to talk in straight language.

10. It gives the opportunity for an abundance of speech-reading practice.

11. It helps to teach geography and history in a casual manner. (While traveling, the teacher marked a map showing the different cities and states that would be visited. Discussing

the different baseball teams and their location also helped the children see different cities.)

12. It lays the foundation for straight language for future years. (Straight language is the crying need of all deaf children. Children started correctly in the early years can avoid many of the language pitfalls so common with older deaf students.)

13. Teaching by this method gives a child an awareness of his environment. Through this motivation language is taught effectively and is a pleasurable experience.

New Words. This is a study of the words used and the number of times which they were used in the news period from October 1 to March 1.

a 120	catch 5	him 12
are 32	camera	he 41
and 40	crew 2	have 43
an 20	circus 3	house bell
at 6	coke 4	happy 28
animals 3	crows 5	had 24
arm 4		her 21
alone 2	does 3	horn 3
apples 2	dark 2	hair cut 4
about 4	day 6	Halloween 3
all 5	did 13	hot 12
ate 6	down	hat 7
also 3	dogs 3	Howdy Doody
airplane 7	Donald Duck 3	house 4
again 6	dinner 2	help 4
aspirin 4	Delmar 5	hearing 5
April 4	doctor 3	helped
another 7	danced	hurts 5
Aunt Helen 2	dancing 2	handkerchief 5
April Fool's Day 2	Dr. Todd 3	hide and seek 5
antenna 3	drinking 2	head 4
	did not 12	headache 4
bracelet 6	Deiter 7	hot dog 3
bed 12	deep	horse
birthday 4	dime 2	hope 3
baby oil 3	Dennison House 4	H Street 4
bread 6	Debbie	hoe 3
Bud Abbot	Deannie	hammer 4
bubble gum	dress 4	helped 3
better 6	darts	here 3
Benny 2	display	hid 2
badge 4	dollar 4	hike 4
brownie 7	dreamed 10	
boat 4	dive	it 34
boats 5	died 2	is 46
ball 8	disappointment 3	ice cream 4

boy scouts 4
boy 24
bit 6
both 4
boys 6
boxed 4
bike 28
black 5
broke 4
basketball 18
bought 12
beautiful 18
bring 5
blue 9
brown 6
bad 16
belt 4
bird 7
birds 8
brought 6
bells 3
button 4
big 5
balloon 7
baby 7
baseball 6
brother 4
back 3
bled 5
burned 7
book 8
boots 4
broken 3
belt
bench 5
bandage 5
bottles 4
Bobby's 10
Brad's 9
Byron's 13

chin 2
cut 4
cake 2
candy 16
cigarette 2
cool 6
comb 4
car 7
costume 3
cowboy suit 3
came 12
cloudy 13
cold 15

daffodils 5
ditto machine
dressed 2
different 3

eye 2
Elmer 5
ear 2
each 3
eating 2
eraser 4
eight 2
enjoyed 4

fell 10
flower 6
fall 3
fix
finger 4
Friday 3
friend 6
four 4
fun 7
feed 6
fed 5
false
father 7
falling 3
fountain
from 3
forgot 4
funny 3
foggy 6
fire 3
for 12
fine 2
first 3
football 2
feel 3
face 4
fixed 2
find 4
foot 5
five
February 3
flew 2
Fabio
feeling 3
flashlight 4
fighting 4
fooled 3

got 6
good 25

in 8
ice skates 4
Indians 3

John 2
jack-o-lantern 3
jet 4
Jack 2
Joe 4
jump 5
Jerry 4
jungle gym 3
Jeanne 5

knife 4
kite 3
kitty 3
knee 4
Kay 3
kissed 3
kitten 4
little 10
leg 3
last 3
lights 4
lighter 3
looks 4
leaves
lightening 2
lettuce 4
like 6
likes 4
lobster 3
letters 3
lost 5
looked 3
Lee 2
Lou Costello
Little Black Sambo
lollipop
lives 3
laws 3
Linda 3
letter 3
lip
learned 3
lizard
lied 4
library 5
love 2
loves 2
laughed 4
long 2

cookies 6
cat 5
comic books 3
cross 2
Charlie Chaplin
cried 5
card 4
camp 2
cry 3
can't 3
Christmas 7
chair 4
cast 2
can 6
calendar 2
coasting 4
cane 2
change purse
cub master 4
chains 3
cub scout 7
cough 5
cocoa
Mr. Peacock 3
Mrs. Von 10
Mrs. Giangreco
maybe
Mr. Young 4
Mrs. Lane 2
Miss Atkins 3
Miss Cabbage 3
Miss West 3
Miss Daniels 2
Miss De Sombre 3
Mr. Wahl 3
Mr. Harry
mean 3
much 2
Macon
Maryland 4
Mickey Mouse 3
March 3
movie pictures 3

not 18
news 2
newspaper 4
new 21
now 4
named 4
nickel 2
nurse 3
nuts
New York 5

green 5
go 6
game 45
get 4
gray 4
God 5
glasses 4
golf clubs 3
golf 4
girls 6
girl 5
gum 6
gun 6
gloves 4
Gene Autry 3
garden 4

hand 3
hurt 16
has 48
hit 19

scratched 7
shined 2
shoes 4
squirrels 3
suit 4
see 6
scared 2
sister 4
silly 3
socks 4
snow ball 3
shirt 4
still 3
swings 7
sweater 4
stockings 2
shot 3
snowman
smelled
smoke
slide 3
sugar
sled 3
shots 2
snow 4
shined 3
sweat
stick
stepped
seesaw
said 3

Martha's 8
mask 4
me 25
man 10
Monday
mother 31
my 26
marbles 4
mustache 3
many 7
made 4
money 5
merry-go-round 3
Mr. Philip
Mr. Turk 10
Miss Walker 5
Miss Rimirez 3
Mrs. Kamala 2
Mr. Giangreco 4
Mr. Delgado 4
mad 4

water 5
wheel
white 8
watch 3
witch 4
were 8
warm 4
window 5
well 7
watched 4
wiggle 2
walking 3
wet 9
Woody Woodpecker 8
washed 2
write 4
won 6
wonderful 5
walk 3
worked 3
wash 3
working
water pistol 3

x-ray 2

you 24
years 3
yellow 7
your 4

on 10
of 3
off 4
October
old 4
our 8
oranges 3
one 3
other 2

pigeon 4
pulled 3
played 72
put 7
pencils 3
peanuts 3
party 4
pieces 3
plant 3
picnic 2
pretty 3
pants 3
painted 4
picture 5
play 4
passed 2
Pokey 5
puppy 2
plaid
pockets 2
pink 3
pennies 3
Popeye 2
pushed 4
punching bag 4
plaques 3
painting 3
Pat
purse 3
plate 2
popped 10
popcorn 11
playing
piece
pop
penny
paper 4
ping pong 3
pledge
picked 2
polo
President Eisenhower
pliers 3

stole 3
spade 2
screw driver 2
sucker
starlings 5
story 3
soldier
spinach 2
strong 2
slingshot
sleeps 2
sleep
sad 5
stomach ache 2
sodas 3
swim 3
sleeping
Santa Claus 6
shorts 4
Sonja 2
Sophie 3
Superman 9
snake 3
suitcase 2
surprise 4

the 45
taking 3
turned 2
two 7
three 7
this 10
too 4
ten 3
turtle 4
threw 2
teeth 2
trees 4
together
take
them 5
thundered 3
tooth
tan 2
turned off 3
3-D 4
turkey 2
turnabout 2
television 13
tumbled 6
tore 3
thumb 3
train 4
toy 4

zoo

will go 47
will begin 3
will feed
will not come 11
will get 3
will meet
will have 4
will make 9
will be 7
will see 5
will paint 3
will thank 3
will eat 2
will ride 4
will learn 4
will rain 5
will bring 6
will fix 3
will come 11
will watch 4
will all go 5
will buy 6
will teach 5
will put 5
will walk 3
will play 6
will read 4
will end
will dive
will not swim
will drive

tomorrow night 7
yesterday 95
last night 70
tonight 15
last week 8
tomorrow 31
yesterday afternoon 62
this afternoon 32
next week 9
this morning 24
last Saturday night 5
this summer 4
Thursday 3
today 26
last Saturday 4
next Tuesday 3
Saturday 4
Thursday afternoon
December
Christmas 5

punished 3
planes 3
polished 2
packed 3

red 8
rode 14
raining 2
rats 8
rained 2
ride 6
ran 2
Roland 2
running 4
roller skates
ring 3
read 6
The Robe 2
raisins 2
rope 4
rang 3
robin 5
root beer 2
rabbit 4
rake 3
radishes 2
rugs 3

sorry 9
sore 3
sick 8
saw 42
some 43
showed 1
such
sun 9
shining 5
she 18
sand 5

tit-tat-toe 3
take 2
talked 5
Three Little Pigs 2
Three Little Kittens 3
target gun
took 3
t-shirt 4
Topper 3
time 4
tennis 3
truck 4
thank you 5
tickets 3
tumble 2
tattletale 2

up 4
us 24
undershirt 5
Uncle Dick
using 3
Union Station 3

very 6
volley ball 4
Valentine Day 3
valentine box 3
valentines 4
vacation 5
Virginia 3
vegetables

we 72
wagon 2
with 32
was 30
weather
watered 6
went 62

Halloween
after a while
last Friday
tomorrow afternoon 5
next Friday

to school 23
to church 14
to the movies 21
to the barber shop 12
downtown 15
to Sunday School 4
to the snack bar 10
home 32
to cub scouts 15
to the chest clinic 2
to the hospital 3
to the dentist 4
to Baltimore 4
upstairs 7
in the snow 2
swimming 18
in the teeth
to South Carolina 3
to North Carolina 3
to New Jersey 3
in the dining room 2
in the bed room 2
to brownie scouts 3
to the store 2
to Kay's house 2
in the basement 5
to the drug store
in the hospital 3
in the circus 5
in the garden 6
in the top bed 2
in the bottom bed 3
in the Hot Shoppe 2

In this list the names of the children were omitted because they were used daily. The pronoun "I" was also left out for the same reason.

The children were also required to write the date daily without help from the teacher.

A description of the weather was written everyday. This also included what might happen in the future. The following terms were used:

The sun is shining.	It is a beautiful day.
It is cold.	It is an awful day.
It is warm.	The sun is not shining.
It is cool.	Maybe it will rain this afternoon.
It is cloudy.	Maybe it will get warm this afternoon.
It is raining.	Maybe it will snow this afternoon.
It is snowing.	It is hot.
It is foggy.	

Junior High and High School

Teaching English to students in the upper areas of our schools for the deaf is a challenge everywhere. It is common knowledge in the field of deaf education that English in every form is a source of constant struggle. So often students who are mature physically and who are interested in more adult subjects are capable of doing only Junior High or Primary work with language. If this level is followed, it is no wonder to any of us that these budding adults develop a dislike for English classes. The following suggestions may aid in overcoming this obstacle. The object of these suggestions is the development of written English through an individualized approach to subjects that would interest a teenager. There is a need to increase general knowledge in these suggestions and as a result of that the student has something to write about that is new and different

to him and thus worth communicating in an interesting way to others. The teacher can set individual goals for the students and, therefore, develop each one more fully. Thus, the possible novelist is able to begin creating his own literary style while the mediocre student strives for simple straight expression.

Textbooks serve only as a crutch in time of need and are not the vital core of the work. Too often teachers tend to push exercise in grammar. The students become *whizzes* in such work easily but still cannot write a few sentences correctly. The constant aim must be to develop the correct written ability in students and not "exercise sharks."

A theme should be due every Monday morning. It should be written in ink on white theme paper following certain rules regarding title and margins. This should be carefully written by the student with consideration given the subject matter, its presentation and grammar. The student should make an outline and rough draft before writing the final draft. At first all themes should be handed in.

The teacher should grade these papers for two things: (1) content and (2) language correctness. The mistakes should be indicated, but, if possible, left for the student to correct himself. When the paper is handed back it should be corrected by the student, checked by the teacher and then recopied to perfection. A paper with less than five minor errors need not be recopied. All themes (the one due on Monday and the recopy) should be saved to determine improvement at a later date.

Themes should be at least two pages in length. (Begin with one page, and work to greater length, if desired.)

Perhaps it will be necessary for the teacher to have individual conferences with each student about his theme. Most of the theme work should constitute homework rather than classtime after the initial program is established. It is a situation for individual improvement with the ultimate goal varying for each child.

The final corrected copy should be finished each week.

SUGGESTED SUBJECTS

1. Read a newspaper item. Rewrite it in your own words.

2. Tell the story of a movie you've seen.
3. Read a magazine story. Write it in your own words.
4. Look at a picture. Write a story (fiction) from what you see.
5. Look at a picture. Write *exactly* what you see.
6. Describe your dormitory room.
7. Describe a building on the campus.
8. Define a word at length.
    cooperation)
    happiness)
    sadness   )
    housewife)
9. Analyze a word or subject.
    sheep - or any one animal
    farmer - or any one job
    magazine for women
    magazine for sports
10. Describe a device
    doorknob
    can opener
    flag, etc.
11. Describe a process.
    making coffee
    making cocoa
    making pie
    making a table, etc.
12. Read a poem. Write your interpretation of it.
13. Read a poem. Discuss it in class, then write about it.
14. Study a graph or table and write your interpretation of it.
    traffic deaths in Iowa
    crime, etc.
15. Evaluate a specific thing. (point out the good and bad)
    car (special make)
    a TV set
    an appliance, etc.
16. Write a book review.
17. State the pros and cons of a problem.
    When shall the teenage begin dating?

Children and TV
Should the voting age be reduced?
Homework done at your discretion or in a study hall?
Should states have speed limits?

Classtime can be related to the theme. Monday will probably be devoted to handing in themes and assigning new ones. The teacher will have to explain what the subject is to be and what that subject requires in regard to research. The object is to make the student increase not only his knowledge of English mechanics, but to learn something on the subject involved so that he increase his vocabulary and general knowledge and so has something interesting, about which he can write. This should develop enthusiasm for the desire to write rather than being mere drill in straight language.

Classes Tuesday through Friday should stress writing well structured sentences on the subject of the week. Writing good paragraphs should then be taught. On some of the subjects a library period, or field trip may be necessary. The field trip will add group activity and group learning to the theme and should give the students guidance in writing their themes individually.

Class discussion and media work should be the key devices. Style individuality should be stressed so that the teacher is developing something the student already has rather than forcing conformity on all the class. Writing style is like a rough stone, "It only needs polishing." No two styles will be alike, but a short correct three or four word sentence is a gem, while a long, incorrect, jumbled sentence is worthless.

When the theme topic does not adapt itself well to the classroom there is the opportunity to bring in related material such as:

1. Everyone describe what other members have on.
2. Write what is seen when looking out the window.
3. Dreams the student has.
4. The seasons.
5. A special event.
6. A gift.
7. Letters.
8. Pets.

This type of subject makes good sentence work and paragraph work.

Another wealth of topic material can come from the senses. Write about something you smell, taste, feel, see, or hear. Use a blindfold in an effort to use only one sense at a time. This can provoke hilarious class periods too:

The sensations from feeling—
> velvet
> fur
> marble
> a rock
> mud
> etc.

The sensations from tasting—
> pickles
> red hots
> syrup
> etc.

The sensations from smelling—
> onions
> roasting beef
> cabbage
> burning rubber
> etc.

The sensations from seeing—
> blood
> raindrops
> snow
> Mother or Dad
> etc.

The sensation from hearing—
> a fingernail on a blackboard
> music
> a jet
> etc.

For vocabulary use a reading series. Start at the preprimer book and go through the entire new word list of each book giving the class ten or so words a day. The students should define the word, if possible, and use it in a sentence. If done correctly, (go on to new words. Words not known are to be taught. The object of this is to create a good basic vocabulary. The Dolch word lists also provide a good guide for essential basic vocabulary. Teaching English in advanced classes need never be a dull, drab chore. Properly taught it can be lively and exhilarating as well as meaningful. All the class needs is the proper guidance and stimulation. This, naturally, should come from the teacher.

A teacher must be lively, friendly and able to get along with ALL the students and have the proper training and background to teach English. An alert teacher must be able to open the doors of learning and find out the interests of each student in the class. This requires understanding the individual needs of each student. A teacher must understand that a student works best when he is doing something that interests him.

When teaching advanced English a teacher should take advantage of every learning opportunity which comes along. English in advanced classes should be correlated with every subject taught. English, written or spoken, is the foundation of all learning; properly taught it can be a fascinating subject.

Reading

Why can't the deaf become better readers? Why are some books too hard for the children to read? Are all the deaf retarded readers?

Teachers continuously ask these and other questions in their quest to teach reading to the deaf. In studying the causes of reading difficulties some interesting facts can be pointed out.

1. Research has proven that there is strong correlation between good reading and good hearing.

"Reading success appears to be closely correlated with language facility and speech. Other things being equal the speed and ease with which children acquire a reading vocabulary is directly related

to the familiarity of the vocabulary content and the breath of meaning behind the speaking vocabulary." (Thompson 1956, p. 7)

2. Reading parents usually help make reading children.
There is a great deal of carryover from a parent's attitude towards reading and the child's attitude towards it. Napoleon once
said,

> "Show me a family of readers, and I will show you the people
> who move the world."

3. Emotional attitude plays a large role in determining
whether or not a child will learn to read.

Taking these three points and applying them to deaf children in a residential school one can easily see that the deaf
child is *reading retarded* before he begins his formal education.
His lack of hearing has deprived him of an opportunity to build
a vocabulary or any form of communication before he enters
school. This is the first major strike against him.

Secondly, the deaf child must live at the school in a dormitory situation which is often not conducive to good reading.
Usually, he is in the care of a house parent who has many children to care for and cannot give the children the proper con-
ditioning for reading.

Thirdly, the child with a hearing defect often has an emotional problem, either minor or of some consequence, due to
his handicap. In addition the fact that school means living away
from home creates another major emotional problem among
younger children.

The above facts point out the problems faced by a teacher
before any schooling has begun. These facts are presented not
as a pessimistic attitude, but to depict the tremendous obstacles
faced by a teacher of the deaf. Thus, deafness presents the most
serious educational handicap of any single physical defect barring
mental problems. In spite of the major obstacles listed above the
deaf DO learn to read and DO hold their own in our society.

Reading is the life line of the average deaf person. Even
though many of them learn to talk, they invariably have to re-
vert to reading because the general public has difficulty understanding speech of the deaf. Reading for pleasure as well as for
work is an important aspect in the training of all deaf children.

Schools for the deaf all over the United States have added special services for practically all phases of deaf education, yet they have often neglected reading, the most important special service. It is time that all deaf educators evaluate reading programs to determine their effectiveness.

To be effective a reading program must answer the following questions:

1. Does it lead lead to the overall development of the child?
2. Does it meet the demands of the child?
3. Does it take into consideration the idea that reading, thinking and language are interrelated?
4. Is the reading program in harmony with the development of the child?
5. Does it consider the dominant characteristics of the child?
6. Is it flexible?
7. Does it lead to independent thinking?
8. Does it take into consideration the slow learner?
9. Does it include different types of reading experiences?
10. Is the program set up so that one can check or test reading results?

The first step involved in teaching the deaf child to read is to build a reading vocabulary to take the place of the hearing child's spoken vocabulary. At this stage a word of caution must be injected. A teacher must use good judgment in making sure that he does not force an immature child to read. Arnold Gesel stated, "Training cannot transcend maturation." Much effective future learning is destroyed when teachers try to force something on a child before he is prepared.

Since a teacher has practically no residual communication with the deaf, the teacher must begin the program by building an extensive vocabulary with the child. In setting up the reading program, nothing should be taken for granted.

Beginning vocabulary should be built-up through association and direct experiences. Cards with names should be placed on everything in the area in which the child spends most of his time. Names of people, parts of the body, clothing, calendar, pictures, toys and other articles should be tagged in a similar way.

Other materials helpful in building a vocabulary include the following:

1. Dolch Picture Word Cards. These cards provide an excellent, attractive and easy way to learn vocabulary.
2. Basic Sight Vocabulary Cards. This type of card can be used for interesting games and for stimulation. For the deaf, especially, establishing a good sight vocabulary is very important for all present and future reading.
3. Sight Phrase Cards are a follow through of the basic sight vocabulary and are a very valuable aid in teaching
4. Group Word Teaching Games.
   reading.
5. Dolch's 2,000 Commonest Words. These help provide strength in word recognition.
6. New media materials.

The use of Dolch materials in a school for the deaf should go a long way in developing the necessary vocabulary to enable the deaf child to begin reading in regular books.

At least the first two years of the child's life in school should be spent building up a large reading vocabulary. A teacher should use any means at his disposal to teach vocabulary.

Once the deaf child's mind is open and communication is developed, the next step is to begin formal reading. At this point an appropriate basic text is essential. In selecting a good basic series it is important that a wise choice be made. Since there are many major publishing firms it is possible to select a basic series which will be of much interest and benefit to the deaf.

In selecting a basic text it is important that procedures followed must be based on a carefully formulated policy which is clearly understood by all who engage in the selection process. All the teachers in a school system should share in choosing a text. Participation in textbook selection by everyone concerned usually results in a better choice and has good by-products which will benefit the child.

After a basic text is adopted it is important to have supplemental readers available. Supplemental readers effectively broaden the child's reading experiences and accommodate individual differences in the event that there are children who do not show an interest in the basic text.

In addition to reading books, schools should be furnished with adequate reading materials to: (1) create an attitude favorable to the use of reading materials, (2) motivate the child to read more, and (3) stimulate a great interest in reading in all subject areas.

Teachers should be taught how to use textbooks more effectively instead of eliminating them. All schools should have adequately furnished libraries which are conducive to good reading.

The school has the responsibility to teach reading. This responsibility is virtually unmatched by any other subject or area. Society relies upon the schools exclusively to teach reading.

In addition to books, there are many other aids which play important roles in the reading process. Since the deaf must rely on their eyes for practically all their reading experiences the use of visual aids can play an effective role in developing reading.

Visual aids make definite contributions to factual aids. Reading, dealing as it does with abstract symbols in the form of words, is especially dependent upon experiential background for understanding. Audio-visual materials help fill in the gaps in the experiential background of the child. They help supply a concrete basis for conceptual thinking.

Conceptual thinking is important in a reading program for deaf children. Teaching the abstract is one of the most difficult phases of deaf education. Since the most of their early training is of concrete nature, the deaf child has difficulty grasping abstract thoughts. Audio-visual aids help clarify abstract thinking by effectively demonstrating what is taking place.

Research shows that a child usually learns more, and retains what he learns longer, when reading is enforced with audio-visual material.

Used effectively, audio-visual aids can help stimulate oral and written expression, and develop descriptive ability. Audio-visual aids have also been effective in developing and sustaining pupil interest.

Audio-visual materials available to teachers include 8mm and

16mm films, slides, filmstrips, transparencies, flat pictures and special machinery for media.

Machinery of special interest in helping a reading program includes the following:

1. Tachistoscope, with a timer. The tachistoscope, although an expensive piece of equipment, used properly can be of much help in a reading program. It can be used to improve attention, accuracy, amount seen in one fixation, speed comprehension and left to right progress. Trained salesmen are available to instruct educators in the operation of the machine. Before purchasing a tachistoscope one should make sure that it will work in the situation for which it is intended.

2. The Controlled Reader aids students by controlling the speed at which they read. The machine's speed can be adjusted to the gradually improving skills of the reading student, however, special training is required to operate the machine.

3. Programmed reading materials can benefit a good reading program for the hearing impaired if teachers screen the materials effectively.

Teachers and administrators in a school system should be familiar with a directory of producers, distributors and manufacturers of special devices to help in a reading program. Maintaining a file of the different types of audio-visual equipment manufactured and catalogs of films which are free, for rent, or for sale is helpful.

Field trips are another aid in the reading process. To the deaf, this medium provides rich experiences. It gives them the opportunity to see first hand what is taking place in different areas of life. Field trips should take in manufacturing plants, muncipal enterprises, museums, art galleries, zoos, etc., and rural activities. Nothing should be overlooked in using this medium for reading instruction. To be worthwhile these trips should be thoroughly planned. Research must be done on a topic before going on a trip, and experience stories should be written when the pupils return. Careful records should be kept of the places visited, reading and planning should be strongly motivated. Time spent on trips, could play a tremendous role in stimulating reading.

Reading is developed through practice. It is important that teachers make classrooms and libraries conducive to good reading by supplying them with many different types of books at all reading levels, reference books, dictionaries, newspapers, magazines, etc. A place should be provided where a child can browse and read whatever he feels like reading. A pleasure reading nook usually takes some of the pressure from reading and the child will usually try to read on his own. The reading area should be kept attractive and as up to date as possible. A librarian should be employed to assist students with their reading problems and selection of reading materials.

The use of diagnostic tests can be used very effectively in helping a reading program. There are many different types of tests on the market today and these can be used in diagnosing reading difficulties, finding reading levels, and isolating weaknesses and strengths in reading.

These tests should be administered and interpreted by a person who has had experience and has a good knowledge of the tests. It is important that these tests be correctly interpreted or they can be damaging. Diagnostic tests are usually kept in the care of an administrator or a reading specialist.

A good reading program should have a complete list of tests available in different areas of testing for reading and should be used to good advantage. A minimum of two tests should be given to children having reading difficulties so that one can be fairly sure of the results.

Today there are many new high interest-low reading vocabulary books in practically all fields of study. The practice has even reached the classics and many of them are being printed in simplified language. These books can be used effectively in stimulating reading and in letting a child feel that he is able to read stories written by some of the great authors. However, children should be encouraged to read from the easy to the more difficult. A child should not become complacent and only want to read easy material. This takes eternal vigilance and careful guidance on the part of the teacher.

There are many materials and instruments which can be used in teaching and recognizing reading difficulties. Caution is again necessary so that whatver is being used does the job that it was intended to do. The following are some criteria for selecting materials and instruments for a reading program:

1. The materials should provide for the development of a systematic sequence of skills.
2. Materials and devices used to supplement the basic program must be specifically related to the particular skill or ability in which the child is deficient.
3. The materials should provide an inherent motivation to read. They should be interesting.
4. Materials used should be varied as to types.
5. Materials should provide a natural approach to reading.
6. In certain phases of the program, materials are effective to the extent to which the child helps to construct them himself.

Any material, device or instrument used is only as good as the teacher using it. Used properly it can be a valuable aid. With improper use it can do more damage than good. A reading specialist could help cure some of the ills which plague the work of the residential school. This person would assume the responsibility of developing and directing a reading program. He would advise teachers and students along reading lines. Working in close alliance with supervisors and principals, the reading specialist could help keep everyone abreast of current reading trends. A reading specialist could become one of the most important people on the staff.

In summary, the following important points are worth review:

1. Immediate and intensive research should be done in the reading area of deaf education to determine the major causes of failure and/or success, and, if possible, answer some of the questions.
2. The entire program in a school for the deaf should be centered around the reading program. Each teacher in the school should be considered a reading teacher and should do his part to help in the venture.

3. Any and all approaches to open the mind of the deaf child should be used in an attempt to stimulate a reading program. This should include audio-visual aids, experience stories, trips, projects, machines and other new equipment coming onto the market.
4. There should be much experimentation in different methods of teaching reading to discover which methods are the most effective.
5. A reading specialist should be a part of every school for the deaf. With the proper training and background this specialist can be of much help and benefit to the deaf child.

Today deaf educators are engaged in a nationwide effort to fit the deaf person into society. Unless they can teach him to read effectively their efforts will be fruitless. Reading is an important part of the deaf person's life. Our job in education is to see that this is done. Education owes to this special group of people at least this much.

One cannot overemphasize the importance of reading. It is continuously stressed in all scholastic activities. It is well understood that the ability to read is probably the most useful tool children can possess. On this ability rests the deaf child's future, his success, and his happiness.

In addition to all the formal reading which is given the children, it is important to also stress the value of recreational reading. In this day of shorter working hours and increased leisure time, recreational reading can help fill many idle hours.

In an article on recreational reading, Miss Eleanor Johnson stressed the fact that free reading is a time when children read without having anyone check on them. It is informal, recreational reading. Its sole purpose is fun. She also stresses that besides enjoyment, free reading helps one become acquainted with their vast literary heritage.

Free reading is a three way responsibility—the library, the school, and the home. Each has an obligation to instill within children a love for reading and the habit of reading. Each has the obligation to help furnish the many books that children need. Parents of students attending schools for the deaf have the same responsibility. The children are home approximately four months each year. During this time it is the responsibility of the parents to surround the child with books making it conducive for the child to read.

Along with fun and play, however, vacation time can also be an excellent time for students to increase their knowledge. Probably the best and most effective way to accomplish this is to read. The public library is a good place for students to visit during the summer months. There children can get good books, read the latest magazines, and look over any new literature.

The average deaf student has difficulty with reading. By taking advantage of every available opportunity to read, the deaf student can improve his reading habits and English usage. It is important for the deaf to raise their reading level because it is their lifeline. Reading also provides excellent entertainment and passes time profitably.

Radio, television, movies and travel also aid the learning process. How much or how little a person learns depends upon his attitude. With the proper attitude and the will to learn, potential learning is unlimited. By making use of leisure time people can gain immensely in knowledge.

Nature study also affords an excellent avenue of learning. Fortunately, many students in Iowa live on or near farms. Life on the farm can provide an excellent education. It gives one an opportunity to study animals, flowers, plants, birds, fish, insects, trees and other natural phenomena. With the proper attitude during the summer months, students can continue to increase their knowledge and enjoyment.

Schools for the deaf can help by bringing libraries up to date and buying attractive books at all levels. If a school does not have a library, one should be started.

Teachers and houseparents can help by encouraging students to read for pleasure. Much time wasted in the dormitories can be utilized by encouraging a sound reading program.

READING, the medium of communication on which the deaf must depend for a livelihood, is also the means by which they can satisfy many leisure hours—hours which can be rewarding and pleasant.

Social Studies

Man, through his creativity, has placed social studies in a new and important position in the modern world. Social studies, once taken lightly by many school systems, has reached a point where everyone must take a critical look at it and re-examine the goals and objectives as the promise of the future. After a thorough examination the necessary steps must be taken to teach social studies in its proper perspective as a guide for living universally.

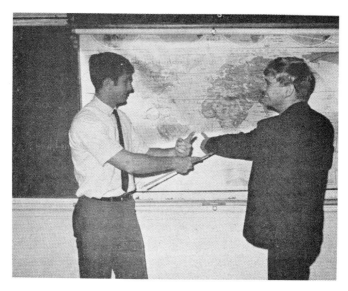

Travel in the United States is possible because modern technology has made it possible for people to travel anywhere in a matter of hours. This same technology has made worldwide travel feasible. Tourist records show that the world is on the move, and yet distant travel is only beginning. Modern space technology has made it possible for men to circle the earth in 90 minutes. Supersonic passenger planes have been developed and will carry passengers around the world.

The Omaha Evening World-Herald of January 21, 1967 carried a story about Eddy Rickenbacker, a pioneer in aviation and automobiles, who, at the age of seventy-six, made the following remarks:

The supersonic transport is bound to come and we will have a break through in atomic power.

We must have the 1,500 to 2,000 mile SST before we can do 3,000 to 5,000 miles an hour with the ramjets.

From there we will go into orbit and we will have rocket airplanes going 10,000 to 15,000 miles an hour.

It will take 15 minutes to fly from New York to London, 18 minutes to Paris, 15 minutes across the North American continent, and an hour at most to go to Australia, halfway around the world. This is in the works. It can and will be accomplished.

Man, not content to develop only transportation, has also joined an arms race. He now has the atomic bomb, the hydrogen bomb and the bacteria bomb, just to name a few. He has weapons at his disposal that can make shambles of our planet. No one nation has a monopoly on these weapons. It is modern man's decision to either enjoy modern technology peacefully or perish from the face of the earth. The choice is his.

Social studies—the study of man, the study of nations, the study of history, the study of geography—is at the core of human existence. We have reached the point of one world. The United Nations is living proof. In New York City, people from the nations of the world are trying to understand each other's problems and trying to help each other. Members of the United Nations cannot do it alone. It is the responsibility of every citizen in the world to take part. It is important that the United States understand people from other parts of the world, and it is just as important that they understand the United States.

It is easy to readily understand the important role which has been thrust upon social studies. With the role, however, have come many problems. Two problems which are especially serious include the following:

1. There is a lack of interest in social studies. Surveys among public school children in the United States indicate that the status of social studies in the secondary school has reached a new low. Students are tired of memorizing long lists of facts and generalizations from textbooks and they have turned their attention to other disciplines that present more stimulating materials or more challenging intellectual experiences. This lack of interest

persists in an area in which the future of mankind is at stake. (Fenton, p. 2)

Indications among schools for the deaf show that social studies apparently is disliked by both students and teachers. Somehow, social studies often has the reputation of a *fill in* subject. Usually all the other classes are scheduled first and then social studies is passed around among different teachers. In many instances, a teacher is not only unprepared to teach the subject, but is also disinterested in it.

2. The reading comprehension of hearing impaired students is limited. Scrutinization of achievement test scores shows a startling similarity between reading ability scores and social studies scores. At the Iowa School for the Deaf, a 1965 research included the following correlations between reading and social studies scores on the Stanford Achievement Test in relation to the Hiskey-Nebraska Test of Learning Aptitude, Revised.

| Grade | SOCIAL STUDIES | READING | |
		Word Meaning	Paragraph Meaning
8	.049	.044	.085
9+10	.246	.211	.175
11+12	.674	.616	.679

Since social studies is basically a reading subject, one can readily accept the above correlations. Social studies becomes a difficult subject initially because of reading problems. Therefore, reading may repel learning in social studies which is taught through the reading medium. Compound the reading problem with the prevailing unfavorable attitude toward social studies and the subject is virtually doomed before the class convenes. The learning theories of educational psychology point out dramatically that the circumstances listed above can only lead to failure.

Perhaps this is a bleak picture regarding social studies in our schools. However, at least one virtue is present—social studies is keeping pace with the students' reading level; maximum use of reading ability is being made. Educators, however, must look beyond reading ability for it alone is not the goal of social studies. What, then, are the goals of social studies? Fenton set forth the following three groups of objectives for social studies instruction:

1. *Knowledge*: The ability to recall or recognize ideas or phenomena that a student has experienced in the same form or in a similar form at an earlier time.
2. *Abilities and Skills*: The ability to find appropriate information and techniques in a student's experience to help him solve some new problems or cope with new experiences. In the social studies, the modes of inquiry of historians and the social sciences are an important part of these abilities and skills.

Affective Objectives: The development of attitude, understanding, and values that will promote a democratic way of life and help each student to develop a personal philosophy.

Recognizing the problems, the challenge becomes one of study in depth beyond learning-through-reading. Decisions must be made concerning educational objectives based on previous experience and aided by consideration of several kinds of data. Teachers should get as much data as they can about the students. They should know their present level of development, their needs, interests, problems which might be encountered and what opportunities they are likely to have for service and self realization. Teachers and students both should understand important values and must consider man's proper relation to society and to his fellow beings.

Every teacher must understand how educational objectives are related to a psychology of learning.

"The use of the psychology of learning enables teachers to determine the appropriate placement of objectives in the learning sequence, helps them to discover the learning conditions under which it is possible to obtain an objective and provides a way of determining the appropriate interrelationships among the objectives." (Fenton, p. 22)

Psychologists with a penchant for systems find a theory of learning essential because so much of man's diverse behavior is the result of learning. If the rich diversity of behavior is to be understood in accordance with a few principles, it is evident that some of these principles will concern the way in which learning occurs.

Teachers must become acquainted with the experiments of Thorndike, Skinner, Guthrie, Koehler, Hull, Tolman, Lewin and

Freud. Each of these men have made definite contributions in the areas of capacity, practice, motivation, understanding, transfer and forgetting. These men, and others, have many proven theses on human behavior and learning. The theorists agree sufficiently upon specific learning areas to make an understanding of learning a valuable teaching aid.

In the study of the learning theories, there are two which are critical—transfer and motivation. Teachers should have some knowledge of the transfer theory to enable them to know and understand some of the knowledge which transfers from one life experience to another. Possibly teachers can devise a method of tying other subjects into the study of social studies. Teachers may also devise a means of presenting material so that it is easily transferable.

Motivation is at the heart of the program. How can we motivate the student to enjoy desire to learn social studies? Nearly all theorists are agreed. Without motivation, there is only a minimal amount of learning. Proper motivation may make it possible for the student to seek the desired direction.

What rewards can we offer the student? Research proves very definitely that reward leads to better learning. If teachers thoroughly study learning theories the desired results may be achieved.

Some of the problems and desired goals have been discussed. To reach these goals, however, is the difficult part of teaching social studies.

It is probable that some people want to find specific teaching aids, such as courses of study, curriculum guidance, films, and textbooks. Materials can be found in the *American Annals of the Deaf, Volta Review, Proceedings of the Convention of the American Instructors of the Deaf,* publishing house materials and other similar sources.

Excellent materials are available. The key to reaching our goals, however, rests in the hands of the teacher and the teacher's ability to be creative as the teacher makes the work meaningful to each *individual* student. The teacher must adapt the material at hand to the student involved. Each situation is one of a kind. For achievement of goals, the teacher must be willing to accept the challenge of assessing each student as an individual entity and determining the student's learning techniques. The teacher must be willing to be uniquely creative in the presentation of materials to be learned so that the student will proceed toward the objective goals. It is impossible to overstress the use of individual media and personal creative innovations as primary teaching aids. Social studies classes should be so interesting that the subject becomes a lifelong interest. To do this requires the use of concepts similar to Pestalozzian philosophy. There must be a natural seizing of the fleeting sparks of curiosity. There must be an awakening of feeling toward the subject. The student must be fed knowledge in tune with his speed and unfolding plan of life.

With this trend of thought you may wonder just how we can assess our progress and determine our success as educators. Test scores on the Stanford Achievement Test and other tests are based on reading. Formal tests should be supplemented by other means to determine success or failure teaching social studies. The real test appears to be the end product of the school—the adult in society.

Iowa is extremely proud of the great successes shown by its citizens who were educated at the Iowa School for the Deaf. They do well and often exceed fondest expectations in the overwhelming majority of cases. These people usually vote in elections, are economically independent, travel, socialize in their communities, become tax payers and contributing members of society in general.

Some of the reasons for the success of these students may lie in the following techniques used in Iowa. Always, there is a striving for improvement upon the situation. There is no simple solution, nor is there total satisfaction with every student's outcome.

Emphasis, however, is on the idea of team—the total school—administrators, teachers, dormitory personnel, maintenance people, cooks, janitors and all employees must realize that the only reason for being on campus is to serve the child so that he becomes an educated acceptable participant in our society both while in school and after he leaves school. There has to be an effective interrelationship among all phases of campus life.

When a child enters school, every effort is made to make the child aware of his environment and help him find his place in home, school, and the community as he relates to other human beings in each circumstance. As he progresses through school, his concern for food, clothing, shelter and money require further learning and development.

As the student grows and matures, he is made aware of extending his world beyond himself. His relationship with others requires realization of the inter-dependence of man and the laws of supply and demand become apparent to him. Recognition of special holidays and observances are a part of the school calendar. The child's enlightment must cover local, state, national, and international affairs. Field trips become a definite part of the program and his awareness of what we commonly consider history, geography, or social studies becomes innate. The student then actually participates in living through doing both in and out of the classroom, at school and away from school.

At school, social studies are taught much of the time through activities. It is common practice to run mock elections which give physical meaning to a national technique used in the United States. Clubs within the school operate on a system of elected officers. Political candidates visit the campus and visit with the students during political campaigns. Every effort is made to visit important political gatherings. For example, students have seen and heard President Johnson, Senator Goldwater, Vice President Nixon, their state governor, state representatives, congressmen and senators. Every two years, junior and senior students take an extended Eastern states trip with at least basic stops in Chicago, Washington, D. C., and New York City. While in the District of Columbia, every effort is made to live and breathe past and present history. Covering the miles by train and bus, participants are continually confronted with the way people live and where they live. Our students have had an opportunity to study life and see the plains, the mountains and the sea along the way. Also, high school social studies teachers have major educational backgrounds in social studies. Teachers use the latest mechanical equipment, film strips, films, magazines, newspapers and textbooks as implements of their teaching.

In summary, here are some "thought starters" for a personal evaluation of school situations.

1. Have you given serious study to educational psychology and, more specifically, to learning theories?
2. Have you considered the success or failure of the social studies program in your school situation by the stature of the end product—the adult in society?
3. Have you explored the vast teaching opportunities and techniques that do not require reading?
4. Have you accepted the challenge to teach each student as a unique individual?
5. Have you established sensible, vital and exciting goals that relate the student to his world?
6. Have you dared to be adventurous and creative as a school, as a teacher and as a class?

Social studies has an extremely vital role to play in everyone's life as they strive for the promise of a better tomorrow. Educators must be innately optimistic, and eagerly accept the exciting and awesome challenge before them by giving their best performance to their students so that satisfying universal living is the final achievement.

Science

Every person should have some understanding of science and how it helps people relate to their environment. Observations constantly are made by everyone. A comparison of details made in observations helps people organize learning. This knowledge helps individuals adjust to the world around them. Thus, culture, the intellectual appreciation of man's surroundings and the joy of knowledge is developed. People must appreciate human behavior and accomplishments and acquire a tolerance and appreciation of others. Science provides a cultural background of truth. Life is a continually changing process and thought must keep pace. There must be a closer understanding with scientific knowledge for successful living.

What should be taught in the realm of science? How should it be taught? In getting acquainted with a new subject it must

be introduced with simplicity. Most students are recipients of scientific knowledge before they meet it formally. Therefore, it is not difficult to introduce formal study based on commonplace knowledge and experiences. This method should automatically

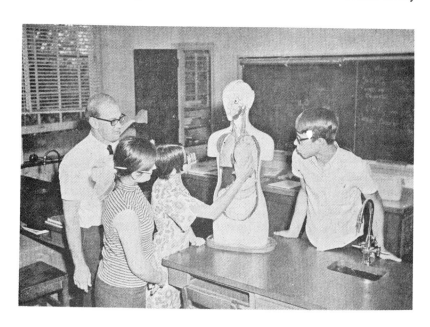

stimulate interest, excitement, and a desire to learn more about science (or any subject). The science program must possess a good structure to insure effective presentation. Text books are not always appropriate, materials often abound with technical

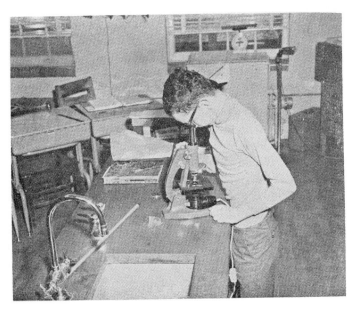

terms. Materials should be presented in an everyday manner; books alone should not be the major resources. Observation and study of phenomena using multi-media materials add much to science programs. Choice of materials should depend upon usefulness with some regard for the ornamental.

There is need for a balance of these two according to Dr. James Conant. Giving subject matter balance will show its interrelatedness which aids the learning process. The curriculum will continually change if it strives to meet the needs of a living and changing complex world. Perhaps an ideal program would involve the *spiral curriculum* in which the material to be learned repeats itself in depth at higher levels. The value of intuition cannot be overlooked in the nurture of learning. Training intuitive thinking is often neglected, but it can be an essential learning tool. The climate of the school plays a major role in the learning situation. The primary agent of instruction, however, is the teacher who must ascertain student readiness so that the structure can be carried out with interest.

In Iowa School for the Deaf science programs evolve with maturation. The kindergarten youngsters are made conscious of their environment as they observe and relate what is around them. Simple projects further the training of observation. Elementary teachers continue the trend and enrich thinking by the use of teaching materials. By the time the high school years are reached students are ready for serious scientific study of the sciences including biology and chemistry.

Science is generally recognized as an important subject and is approached with a serious desire to learn. Iowa teachers are well trained and enjoy their subject. Materials and laboratories are available to do an effective job.

Science has come into its own with about 90% of all the scientists who have ever lived being alive today. New and exciting horizons confront us everyday so it is no wonder that the excitement of science catches hold of students and learning takes place. Schools for the deaf are not different in this respect.

Mathematics

New math, modern math, old math, regular math are terms tossed about in educational circles as curriculums are discussed. Some schools have jumped into extreme programs and perhaps jumped out just as fast. Some schools feel the latest trends are beyond comprehension and do not bother to explore the possibilities. Transition programs are still another trend. A few schools have successfully updated mathematics programs so they embody both the old and new ideas. Degrees of change are multitudinous. The point remains that mathematics is a subject under scrutiny and undoubtedly will come out with a different face even though the features are far from absolute.

Schools for the deaf also feel the surgence of change. Teachers are interested in the latest trends and strive for what is best for the students. Criteria for educators involved in a math program should include the following ideas: (1) It is important that the learner have experiences of a concrete nature so that future abstractions can have a firm base. A working knowledge of mathematics is essential.

J. Bruner says that four aspects of teaching are essential—discovery, intuition, translation, and readiness. Teachers must stimulate the quest for knowledge and a good teacher can provide experiences that demand proper responses. Students can become aware of concepts intuitively before they have terminology for the concept. Translation refers to the need to state things so that ideas can be converted to mathematical expression. This involves transmitting knowledge and ideas in language that is understandable to the student. Finally, readiness is not so much a function of maturation as it is expressing ideas at the proper level to permit comprehension.

With the preceding thought in mind it is necessary to decide what will be taught. Knowledge is doubling itself every seven years. It is impossible to teach everything in the accepted length of school calendars. Therefore materials must be sorted for the greatest possible good. The only possible solution, according to Bruner, is to seek out the relatedness of material so that a student will discover for himself what is worth knowing. Any knowledge chosen as necessary to be taught should give a sense of delight and bestow the gift of intellectual travel.

The type of approach to be given to mathematics can be decided after thinking through some of these basic ideas. In schools for the deaf mathematics teaching is one of the brighter spots of achievement, for students tend to comprehend and move at a rate which compares favorably with regular schools. Teachers of the deaf have long recognized the need for a concrete foundation with progressive steps to semi-concrete, semi-abstract, and abstraction. These four levels of difficulty progress from the easiest and are recognized necessary steps of learning. There must be involvement with the subject by the students so that learning takes place. Knowing these things and having them in practice makes the choice of mathematic instructional materials somewhat easier. The latest trends easily fit into programs, providing the trends meet the criteria of being valuable to the existing program. Established methods need not be abandoned simply because they are old. They, too, must be useful as the mathematics curriculum meets the needs of relationships essential for pursuing learning. If they do, there is no need to discard them.

Critical evaluation is at a peak in mathematics. The stress and strain of programs can only lead to the eventual wholesome selection of materials and ideas that will further the needs of mankind in his search for meaningful, useful knowledge.

Guidance

All of education has become aware of the needs of guidance and steps have been taken to meet at least some of the goals of guidance. Essentially all of education is a form of guidance, but special problems have arisen in schools necessitating inclusion of guidance counselors as part of the school staff.

Ideas pertaining to the nature of man differ, and the whole goals of life therefore vary from individual to individual. Individuals must be able to examine themselves and then figure out a working relationship with society, so that they can get what they desire in life. People cannot live in total isolation, and so individuals must find themselves as they learn to relate to others.

In any type of counselling one of the big problems is communication. Different generations see things differently. Diction-

aries show various meanings for any given word. Therefore, communication and comprehension are primary concerns of guidance work. This leads to the need for specially trained people in guidance work. In schools for the deaf a psychological guidance background is important, but it must be supplemented by

an understanding of the hearing impaired if full utilization can be realized. Counselling duties should be clearly defined. Counselors should be secure individuals with clear concepts of their own values and an awareness of their own skills and abilities. A counselor must give the idea that he really *cares* about the individuals he works with. Individuals must be given the freedom to grow and the help to perceive what they are doing so that they can accept responsibility for themselves and others. There is an obligation to prepare a person so he can be an effective member of society.

Guidance in three areas helps meet the needs—personal, vocational and a guidance class. The requirements of these three areas include extra staff people and time inside and outside the classroom. Very likely a man and a woman are needed to deal with the peculiar personal problems of boys and girls. All children should have access to the people working in guidance and, of course, the size of the school would determine the number of counselors needed.

The vocational counselor has the job of visiting with older students to help establish realistic scholastic goals with an after school vocation in mind. Further, aid in on-the-job training, visits to industry and other work situations, post high school education and finally, job placement are all areas of consideration for the vocational counselors.

A classroom approach can be a useful means of aiding high school students in many of the particular problems which everyone faces in adulthood. Possible subjects to be included in such a course are as follows: heredity, first jobs, budgets and buying, credit, establishing a home, money and banks, investments, insurance, taxes, doctors and dentist, and contacts with the law.

Another group approach in guidance can be used to teach social hygiene. This would probably function best as a subject for smaller more informal groups than might be necessary to cover the previously mentioned topics. In the area of social hygiene, topics to be discussed might include social growth and development, dating, marriage and the family.

An effective guidance program in a school helps prepare better graduates as the students are able to be realistic about themselves and their future because of the opportunities for learning and self evaluation made available within the school.

Vocational Training

During the past few years, there have been rumblings about the residential school to the effect that too much time has been used up in vocational training. It has been pointed out that students were beginning their vocational training too soon and were going to the shops too often.

Many of the critics felt that academic achievement in the residential school would be higher if more time would be spent in pursuit of academic training. These critics also contended that the residential schools were losing many potential college students, because too much time was being spent in the shops.

Finally, with the strong emergence of state and federal departments of vocational rehabilitation, critics claimed that there was too much duplication going on. They felt that it might be a good idea to let the State Department of Vocational Rehabilitation take care of trade training after the student had left the school.

A study completed in 1959 at the Iowa School for the Deaf, showed that a great majority of former students of the Iowa School for the Deaf were *not* following the vocational field in which they specialized while in school. Of 132 responses to a questionnaire which was sent out, only 21 or 15.9 per cent were in occupations which used the vocational field in which they had the most training. These circumstances could have resulted from a lack of vocational opportunity, a lack of personal interest in that particular vocational field, or many other factors.

Those in favor of a strong vocational program contend that the important thing is teaching the use of tools and not student proficiency in one specific area. They feel that transfer to another area will come easier even though a person is not trained in a specific job. These people feel that it is important to maintain a strong vocational program.

Today, it is important that everyone connected with the residential school take a long look at the role of vocational training for the deaf. The following are some of the considerations to be made:

1. A strong academic program should predominate. A student able to handle this program should take only a token amount of vocational training. College emphasis should be stressed with these students and everything should be done to give them a good foundation for college.

2. More use should be made of aptitude tests to determine where a student's strength lies. These tests, if administered properly, can be strongly used to show a student his best fields of interest.

3. Proper counseling should be an important part of this program. For example, too many students and parents are more interested in having furniture built, rather than learning a trade. Many look at the high salaries printers are making in deciding on which trade to study. Very few are asking themselves whether or not they have the aptitude and intelligence for a certain occupation. (This may be a major factor as to why students do not follow the trades they study in school.)

4. Opportunity should abound for the vocational student to learn a good trade.

5. Students should not just be put in a class to fill it.

6. Efforts should be made to reduce the existing duplication by school vocational programs and the state departments of vocational rehabilitation.

The Iowa School for the Deaf, has taken a critical look at its vocational program and schedules were modified accordingly.

For example, vocational training for some youngsters was cut in half. Training for some others was doubled. More care was used in placing students in shop assignments. Vocational and academic teachers worked more closely together in all areas to see how they could help each other.

Modern times and technologies are changing rapidly and it is important that our vocational departments keep in step with the latest trends.

The vocational department of any residential school for

the deaf is an integral part of the school and the child's education. By using care, caution, and just plain common sense, there will be no wasted time, no duplication, and a program will be provided to take care of the needs of *all* the students.

An article by the economist, Sylvia Porter, pointed out some facts which are worth pondering:

1. Today in the United States 30 per cent of the unemployed are under twenty-five years of age.
2. The jobless rate among the *young, uneducated, unskilled* American is by far the highest of any group.
3. The unemployment rate among high school drop-outs is double that of high school graduates.
4. *Forty per cent* more Americans will become job seekers in the next decade.

At the same time that the above statistics are taking place, *the demand for skilled workers will rise to an all time high.* In the next decade there will be a minimum need of 5,000,000 additional *skilled workers* to carry on normal activities. As one looks at these figures, one sees a fantastic paradox. On the one hand there will be *critical unemployment among the unskilled,* and at the same time there will be a *critical shortage of skilled workers.*

Deaf educators must look at the above statistics objectively and turn out more highly educated and better skilled students to fill what needs may be available.

It means that students and teachers must work harder in both the academic and vocational departments to turn out students who can think, can read and write with accuracy, can make good use of time, have the proper attitude both on and off the job, and to take advantage of whatever opportunity may come their way.

It also means that educators should all examine the vocational departments critically to determine their departments' abilities to meet today's demands. Too many schools are living in the past, and their vocational shops are set up exactly as they were many years ago.

Advancing technology has created the need for shops alterations to meet the changing times. Only in this way will students be able to cope with the challenge that they will face.

In her article, Sylvia Porter mentions a few more ideas which are applicable to the deaf, and the hearing:

1. Students are going to need much more guidance on individual, community, and national levels for getting the maximum training possible. In this guidance students should be warned that without ample skills they will *start and stay at the bottom.* Pound home just the facts which are mentioned in this article and you will be achieving a great deal.

2. Build up the idea to the student of becoming a skilled worker. Point out that a skilled worker is very essential to the economy of our country and that jobs are plentiful for this type of person.

3. *Make students realize that it is a tragic error to quit school when they have the ability to complete their education.*

In preparing students many times we fail to take into consideration the factor of *personality.* Personality plays an important role in everyone's lives. Many times it is not the amount of knowledge a person possesses, but his ability to get along with his fellow man harmoniously.

S. and E. Duvall, in a recent newspaper issue, stated that a survey of 3,607 men and women, who had lost their jobs showed that 77 per cent had been fired because of personality defects and a *lack of understanding of people.* The article further stated that success today requires technical competence and good mental health. Understanding one's self and others is usually more important than good technology.

The importance of the above statement should be told students working for the first time. A high quality of work, cooperation with fellow workers, friendliness are essential to good mental health and success in a job.

The following are some of the occupations which were reported at a recent Iowa School for the Deaf Homecoming: truck driver, cobbler, upholsterer, file clerk, typist, IBM operator, business man, book binder, teacher, farmer, aircraft worker, rubber factory worker, glass factory worker, barrel factory worker, plastic factory worker, stock clerk, janitor, maid, power sewing machine operator, auto body and fender repairman, leather worker, linotype operator, presser, cabinet worker, baker, laundry worker, pressman, radio and tube factory worker, programer for computer.

It is a good feeling to know that these former students integrated into society. Society gave these deaf and hard-of-hearing students the opportunity to receive a formal education. These former students are repaying society by becoming solid, taxpaying, self supporting citizens.

Dormitory and Extra Curricular Activities

Though most educators of deaf students are trying to prepare deaf children to fit into a hearing society, segregation of the sexes is practiced in social relations on the campuses of many residential schools for the deaf. Students completing their education are then expected to have no difficulty dealing with both sexes when living on their own in society.

After working in residential schools for the deaf, this author found no valid reasons for the extreme segregation and sought outlets for more social freedom for the students. More social contacts in a controlled school situation should ease students' adjustments to society.

The Iowa School for the Deaf began a number of bold experiments several years ago. The situation for experimentation presented itself when a number of students asked why they could not date the same as their hearing counterparts. Secondly, many students were openly breaking rules and regulations which, when studied closely, were found to be unusually restrictive.

A teachers' committee, a student committee and a parents' committee were established. These committees all examined the idea of allowing the students to date. Many joint committee meetings and individual caucuses were held. The unanimous conclusion was that students should be given an opportunity to date on a controlled basis. This reply was given to the administration and upon careful consideration was approved.

The committees then set up the program on a working basis. They drew up rules and regulations to guide the program.

Dating privileges were started on a trial basis only. If they were abused, they would be stopped immediately. Before students were allowed to date, a copy of the rules was sent to the parents and the parents gave written consent for their child to participate. The student was given a copy of the rules to study. After he had time to study the rules, they were explained thoroughly. The student and the parents kept their copies for reference so there was no excuse for ignorance of the rules.

When the program began, only the seniors were allowed to date. This gave the administration an opportunity to study the reaction from all points on a limited basis and to see what changes in the regulations might need to be made. The student reaction was one of joy and after the first year, the entire school knew it was on the right track. During the second year, dating privileges were given to juniors also. Again, the students showed that they were deserving of the program. Now the class barrier has been dropped completely, and any students who are sixteen years old or older may date.

The students have had dating privileges for many years now and so far there have been few infractions. Although it is hoped that this record will continue, it is apparent that there could be some difficulties. In spite of that, dating has come to the Iowa School for the Deaf to stay. Interesting observations from the program include the following:

1. Teenage students are living a more normal life than they did in the past.
2. The students are happy with the arrangement and try hard to uphold the trust which everyone has placed in them.
3. There is no more sneaking around, which leads to trouble, as there was in the past.
4. It gives younger students something to look forward to.
5. Retraction of dating privileges is an effective disciplinary measure.
6. Parents are pleased that their children are learning to date in a controlled situation.
7. Students feel that dating privileges eliminate one more thing that makes them different from hearing high school students.

The dating program has proven itself so successful that the administration decided to relax other restrictions that had grown up with the school over the past one hundred years. The following have been accomplished:

1. Older students are allowed to mix in the dining room. The seniors may pick their meal partners. This has done wonders toward the improvement of table and social manners.
2. A Sunday evening social program was started, in which the students plan their own programs in conjunction with the recreation workers. Rarely are any two evenings alike.
3. Co-educational recreation programs were begun. Swimming, volleyball, gymnastic shows, croquet, table tennis, and many other activities were organized, and both boys and girls take part.
4. Students are allowed to date for movies and some parties held on the campus. For the movies, the balcony of the auditorium is reserved for couples only.
5. Students are allowed to walk around the campus holding hands if they wish.

The greater majority of the students have accepted their

new freedom with appreciation. The students themselves help to keep each other in line should any begin to take advantage of their freedom. They do not want to lose any of these privileges which they enjoy so much.

It has taken thought and organization on the part of the administration, faculty, counsellors, parents, and the students themselves to bring about these changes. In many cases it took real courage to break ancient traditions. However, the changes in social regulations have not been regretted.

An extra-curricular activities program is a necessity for residential schools for the deaf. Students need to have available constructive activities to which they can devote leisure time. A sound recreation program can fill this need for every age bracket in the school.

Many schools end the academic day for primary age children at two o'clock and the children are left to create their own recreation until mealtime.

The academic day ends at three-thirty for older children in most schools. Unless there are varsity athletics, the free time between school and dinner becomes a time for dreaming up mischievious activity.

Weekends present still another problem of too much time. After the routine chores are completed, there is nothing to do and the children become bored, unhappy and listless.

At the Iowa School for the Deaf, the administration has recognized the existence of this unfortunate situation and has atempted to eliminate it. First a recreation director was hired. The person chosen had been a teacher in the academic area who was familiar with the students and who was genuinely interested in their welfare. In this case the person was a young man who was willing to give unselfishingly of his time when the program required unusual hours. He had been on the school staff for several years and so was familiar with school policy and was understanding of the basic school philosophy.

Secondly young houseparents with good backgrounds in physical education and recreation were hired. These people worked directly with the recreation director. Fortunately it was possible to find young people who had just graduated from college or who were in their senior year. To make their salary satisfactory these people were part-time teachers and counselors.

In addition to the houseparents, part time recreation workers were hired who were present for certain after school hours and on weekends.

With a director and capable assistants the school recognized the need for adequate equipment and this soon became a sizable item in the school budget, but with the personnel to carry out the program and the value of seeing equipment in actual use, it was soon purchased.

The staff is capable and the program is set up in the following manner: (1) All students who are not participating in varsity athletics, are required to become a part of the recreation program. (If there is no varsity practice, the entire student body participates.) (2) Daily from three forty-five to five o'clock there is some activity in session. (3) Every evening recreation is available from seven thirty until nine. (4) On weekends, a schedule is posted.

Available recreation activities include the following: touch football (older students), midget football (younger students wearing pads), volley ball, basketball, swimming, field trips (zoo, wrestling matches, ice capades, Mardi Gras, Offutt, Boys Town, art museum, museums, Christmas decorations), social hours, clubs, billiards, table bowling, table tennis, handcrafts, badminton, baseball, midget baseball, softball, tennis, croquet, hiking, parties, pep squad, dances, dramatics, track and field.

Teams were organized in the different events and competition was keen. In some cases small prizes were awarded; the students were all enthusiastic.

The following are some of the results that have been seen in the operation of this program:

1. All the students are taking part in some constructive phase of the program. Students not able to participate in varsity athletics find their niche which boosts their personality development.

2. Students recognize and accept responsibility by helping plan some of the activities. They also act as scorekeepers,

referees, umpires, and as big brothers and sisters to the younger students.

3. The students seem much happier. They are not as lonely, are less homesick, and don't have too much time on their hands.

4. There is more mixing of boys and girls in group activities at all age levels. They swim together, play volley ball, badminton, tennis, croquet, and other games together.

5. There is more interest in the community as a result of the many field trips taken. The students go to the Saturday night wrestling matches, special movies, ice capades, museums, parks, zoos, picnics, Boys' Town, and Offutt Air Force Base. The students know and appreciate what a community has to offer. And the public become aware of the deaf. (Our students have always had a schedule for going to town for shopping or movies. The younger students go with their houseparents and the older students have more freedom. These trips are scheduled on Friday night, Saturday afternoon and evening, and Sunday afternoon.)

The attempt at a rounded recreation program is just one phase of the work in Iowa in our effort to educate the *whole* child. This is a very important phase, for it develops personality, promotes socialization and physical welfare, and makes a healthier and happier child.

The goal of all schools for the deaf is to prepare the deaf child for the hearing world. Schools for the deaf are doing an adequate job scholastically. Upon graduation, nearly every student is able to find work and settle down in a community. In talking to deaf adults, however, one gets the feeling that the deaf person is often insecure in his hearing environment. He seems to retire from hearing people—is lonely and at times afraid to make friends with hearing people. The result of this tends to be that the deaf adult gradually drifts toward other deaf people and they break away from the social life of the hearing society. Socially—the deaf feel ostracized from the hearing world for which they were raised to live in and in which they *must* live.

Analyzing the school is basic to understanding this situation.

Social customs of hearing people should be taught through actual experience with hearing people.

The Iowa School for the Deaf has established a program to bring about a better understanding between hearing and deaf people. Some of the following are ways in which this is accomplished:

Y-Teens—The older girls are a part of a national program. As part of the program, the girls meet with girls of the Council Bluffs high schools. These activities include teas, skating, parties, dances, etc. During summer vacation some of the girls attend Y-Teen camp.

Scouting—The boy scouts go on camporees with hearing boys. They must compete for awards and honors. In addition, joint meetings and recreational activities are held with troops in Council Bluffs.

Athletics—The girls and boys play varsity and junior-high athletics against hearing teams. The program gives the public an opportunity to see boys and girls in action. In addition, students have the opportunity to travel around the State of Iowa, and mix with hearing people.

Trips—Probably the highlight of the students' life at I. S. D. is the biennial Eastern states trip. This trip serves to help the students mix with hearing people on trains, busses, hotels, restaurants, etc. Students are exposed to the world on this trip and it helps serve educational social experiences. It also plays an important role in the overall development of the child. In addition to this extended trip, many short field trips help create good contacts with hearing people.

Mardi Gras—Each year, four of our students take part in the Mardi Gras which is held in Council Bluffs. In this, students from I. S. D. are mixed with hearing students from the Council Bluffs high schools. All reports point out that the children have a good time and meet many new friends.

In looking over the total picture of relations between the deaf and hearing, it is plain to see that the public is ignorant of problems that deafness creates. By mixing the deaf with hearing people, some of this ignorance can be eradicated. The deaf owe it to themselves to be friendly with hearing people. By doing so, the deaf will be happier, feel a part of the community, and can truly participate in the hearing world.

HIGHER EDUCATION

After graduation from high school the hearing impaired student is prepared to continue his education or work. If a student chooses a vocation, many possibilties present themselves in trade schools or business schools.

Opportunities for a higher academic education for students unable to attend regular colleges are limited to two institutions, Gallaudet College in Washington, D. C., and Rochester Institute of Technology, Rochester, New York. Gallaudet College, established by Abraham Lincoln in 1864, is a liberal arts college.

Rochester Institute of Technology incorporates the National Institute for the Deaf. Established by Congress 1965, this institute of technology offers deaf students educational and technical training.

Chapter IV

POST-SCHOOL THOUGHTS

THE DEAF AS SUCCESSFUL ADULTS

On AUGUST 23, 1962, the Associated Press carried across its wires the story of Shirley McLeland. The story is one with a happy ending and points out that in spite of a severe hearing loss Shirley was able to graduate from college, work for a United States Senator, enter graduate school, become a teacher,

and enjoy most of the benefits which society has to offer. In one way or another, Shirley's success story has been repeated by many others who have gone through the doors of the Iowa School for the Deaf. Like Shirley, others have graduated from college and have successfully entered the ranks of different professions. Those who have not gone to college have entered a variety of occupations. In one way or another all have become contributing members to a society which had faith in them.

Success does not come easy to the handicapped. Success to the hearing handicapped comes even harder. In many instances these handicapped people are prejudiced against in their own homes, among their own families, in business and industry, and among the general public.

To be a successful handicapped person, therefore, requires that the four ingredients mentioned above be favorably mixed together. That is, the handicapped person, the parents, the school, and the community all must work together to bring it about.

The principal actor, of course, is the student. The student must have the ambition, the drive, and the proper attitude which is necessary for success. This is the student who does more than the minimum, and who is always anxious to do all that he can to make himself a better person and his school a better school.

The parents must be able to accept the handicapped child for what he is. This means that the child is to be neither spoiled, nor neglected. The child must be treated as a member of the family, and included in all family activities. The child must be able to feel that he is loved, accepted, and wanted by his family. Parents must have confidence in the school which is educating their child; this means cooperating with the school in helping to make the child a better child.

The community plays an important role in a child's development. Sadly, this phase of development is greatly neglected. The community must be willing to accept the handicapped child just the same as it would any other child. This means that the deaf child should be given the same opportunity to work at part-time jobs, be a part of a recreation program, and take part in all social functions. The deaf child must also be accepted kindly by neighorbors and merchants and made to feel he is wanted.

The school must be prepared to give each child the program to which he is best suited. This may mean a great deal of extra work, but it will also help meet the needs of many students who would be in danger of neglect. The school should be prepared to help develop the child mentally, physically, and socially. The school should make it possible for the students to enjoy the *art of learning* and the *art of living*.

On Sunday, November 22, 1960, the Council Bluffs Nonpareil ran a full page of pictures on its society page showing different families preparing for Thanksgiving. By looking at the pictures, one could not tell that all the families shown were deaf.

The Nonpareil went out of its way to prepare this page and to show the public how deaf families planned to spend the holidays. It made a very interesting page.

While the pictures were being taken, a reporter asked these people what they had to be thankful for this Thanksgiving Day. The answers were many: citizenship, wonderful parents, good jobs, children, plenty of food, good homes, material things (cars, cameras, furniture, etc.), good neighbors, hearing aids, churches, recreation, happiness, Iowa School for the Deaf, good health.

All the families interviewed had something to be thankful for and were very appreciative of the many things which had been done for them while in school.

The Iowa School for the Deaf is thankful that most graduates can leave school and become happy, self supporting, tax paying, contributing members of society. Iowa School for the Deaf is also thankful that its graduates go out into the world and enjoy the same benefits as those enjoyed by other people.

The Iowa School for the Deaf has no monopoly on what is being done all over the United States. Schools similar to this one across the nation are doing their share in educating the deaf and sending them out into the world as productive citizens.

The Deaf in Society

The Deaf—a group of people with a handicap who really are not *handicapped*.

Deafness strikes a cruel blow to the organism in the area of learning. In order to appreciate the educational obstacle which a deaf person faces, we must backtrack and start at the beginning of his educational program.

A hearing child who enters kindergarten has a working vocabulary of over 5,000 words. All of these are learned through the ears. He can say many of these words and understand many of them by hearing them. The deaf child age five, however, enters school with a minimal vocabulary. The teachers must start to teach him their names, names of their family, parts of the body. While the deaf child is learning the few basic words in life, the hearing child is advancing by leaps and bounds. This can aid in pointing out that the educational gap between the hearing child and the deaf child increases, rather than decreases, as the schooling continues.

Educationally speaking, how crippling is deafness? Aristotle, one of the first to comment, pointed out that the deaf could never learn because they could not hear. Throughout the years many other educational leaders have carried on the same theme. Stroud, of the State University of Iowa, pointed out that there is definite correlation between intellectual ability and listening ability. The correlation is so strong that he predicts that intelligence evaluations can be made by listening tests alone.

In spite of what the so-called experts point out, our schools are reaching and teaching the hearing handicapped. They are learning to read, to write, to talk, to study, and to carry on educational curricula similar to those of public schools.

To compensate for the some limited achievement, a strong effort is made to train the student in some vocational trade. In this, schools for the deaf have made valuable and lasting contributions. Today, when the hearing handicapped student finishes school he is able to take his place in society and make a contribution to society, repaying the taxpayer for his investment in deaf education.

What kind of work is the deaf person able to do? A study by Drake in 1968 shows that the deaf in Iowa are employed in the following occupations:

Printing (all areas)
Photography (film processing, offset)
Automotive (body rebuilding, painting, trim work)
Carpentery (home building, commercial building, cabinet making)
Upholstery
Leathercraft
Business occupations (key punching, filing, typing, accounting)
Tailoring

Welding - production
Machinists
Drafting
Electronics (radio and television repair, assembly line work)
Farming
Manufacturing (tire and rubber, John Deere, etc., fabrication plants, etc.)
Textile industry (machine operators, etc.)
Unskilled (hatchery workers, food processing, maintenance work, assembly
line work)
Teaching
Library work

In Omaha, at the Disbrow Company, 15 percent of the employees are deaf. Serta has a large percentage of deaf, as well as Pendleton, Campbell Soup, and Mastercraft.

The deaf are employed in any type of work which does not require hearing. More highly educated deaf are making valuable contributions in the Space Program at Cape Kennedy and White Sands, New Mexico. Those without hearing make it possible to perform experiments which are too painful to hearing ears. One can see that the deaf fulfill economic needs and become hardworking, taxpaying citizens.

In regard to adjustment in communities, the deaf have difficulty in making friends with hearing people because in most instances hearing people won't take the time to become acquainted with them. The deaf are warm, friendly people and will welcome friendship.

The deaf are a proud group; they ask no charity. All they ask is to be given an opportunity to make a living, raise a family, and to become active members of a community.

Help for the Adult Deaf

Today among the adult deaf population there are some who have not had the opportunity to attend school. Some reasons are as follows:

1. Parents kept them at home rather than send them to a residential school.
2. Some were sent to institutions other than a school for the deaf.
3. Some sat in public school classes, not benefiting.
4. Some were not permitted to attend school because school officials did not want to be bothered.

These circumstances have resulted in a certain segment of the deaf population walking around unemployed, unable to read or write; the prey of many unscrupulous people and still in many cases, the responsibility of society.

In order to help alleviate this condition, Congress, in 1962 through the office of Vocational Rehabilitation, authorized $243,350 to be spent over a four year period to help these unfortunate adults.

Beginning in 1962, funds were provided for a residence center that will eventually serve between thirty and forty people. It will have seven employees.

The project began as a means to rehabilitate deaf men who have never gone to school, those with multiple handicaps, and those who, for one reason or another, could not hold a job. Training was on a personal and pre-vocational level and upon completion, the men were referred to Vocational Rehabilitation.

For the future, however, this points out some of the weaknesses of our present day schools which must be remedied. It is the duty of the schools to prevent the deaf from reaching such a sad state of affairs that Congress must rescue them in adulthood.

Schools should do such things as:
1. Provide for better public relations so that everyone will know the function of the residential school for the deaf.
2. Make provision for *parental* counselling. Parents must be made to understand some of the implications of "deafness". They should not only be told about the present, but also what lies in store for the deaf adult.
3. Sound field work is a "must". Every school or state agency should have a field worker who understands the problems of the deaf. This worker should be ready to check out every suspected case of hearing impairment and prepare the child and family for school.
4. Schools for the deaf should be prepared to fit their program to the needs of the child.

Some people forget that schools for the deaf are established to serve the students. If a student doesn't measure up to a certain IQ or has some other simple handicap, he is rejected.

Though many of these students have no place to go, educators reject them without trial, failing to realize that maybe their measuring instruments were not valid.

If all schools for the deaf would assume the basic responsibilities which is theirs, there would be less of the problem which now exists among the adult deaf. Much of the suffering among these people would be alleviated if schools did their job before these humans reached adulthood.

If all schools for the deaf would pitch in and do the job, this problem could be solved for future generations, and, the adult deaf and the taxpayers would both benefit.

Chapter V

SPREADING KNOWLEDGE
TO PARENTS
AND THE PUBLIC

HEARING HANDICAPPED CHILDREN NEED
UNDERSTANDING

One OF THE MORE unpleasant duties of deaf educators is listening to parents discuss the difficulties of their family relationships due to the presence of a hearing handicapped child.

Anyone who is the parent of a handicapped child knows that there are innumerable problems and ideas that must be oriented in the parents' mind when the news of the handicap of the child is first announced to them. After the initial shock and attempt at orientation is over, the realities of the situation are faced.

One of the first things any parent probably hears is that they should treat the deaf child the same as any other child. (This is almost a universal statement in much literature written for parents.) With the best of intentions, people involved in this field of endeavor may have minimized the differences of a hearing handicapped child to such a degree that the inevitable special problems surprise and frighten parents to such an extent that the parent-child relationship soon deteriorates and there exists an unseen barrier in the family. In an attempt (and an honest one, too) to treat the child as hearing offsprings the parents soon find that the results are different. The deaf child doesn't seem to care. The deaf strays away from the family group. These are what an administrator hears all too often. Other parents wait patiently for their child to suddenly come home from school and be a part of the family, and when he doesn't it is bitter disappointment so that only bits and pieces of an inadequate relationship can be picked up. The *situation puzzle* always has too many pieces.

A study of the situation resulted in some observations and findings that may be of interest to others.

Parental Attitudes

Initially, there are several basic facts that should be considered. The parent of any atypical child may be overzealous and show a special eagerness that may cause an unnatural quality in the parent's personality. Parents often admit being anxious or concerned about deafness. This may or may not be sporatic, but it appears especially in times of stress of the child. Oftentimes the problem is confused because it is not easy to determine whether the child's difficulty is due to age, or his handicap.

Often, many parents forget that all children can be exasperating, demanding and remarkably unlovable at times, while many parents feel harried and overburdened occasionally. Parents of deaf children react with guilt to a momentary, or sometimes more permanent, dislike of the child, and wonder if they have some kind of hidden or not so hidden negative feelings about the child. Finally, in any family there are differences in temperament, talents, and interests, regardless of what parents are like.

With these ideas in mind, it is important to re-emphasize that in our eagerness to soothe over the initial anguish of learning that a child is deaf, the parents are all too often told to treat the child as if he has no problems—"treat him just like the other children in the family." This is no doubt done with the best of intentions, but it seems that this is the beginning of the downfall of the parent-child relationship. It is misleading and actually countenances a falsehood to say first that the child doesn't hear well and then turn around and tell the parent to assume there is nothing wrong with him. It is because of this initial direction that we then have parents unprepared for the special problems and the later shock and surprise and general inability to cope with the situations which arise. *Deafness does make the child different.* If he were not different parents would not have reason to seek medical and educational help. Although he requires the same love and care that any child needs, there is need for special consideration by the entire family circle if the child is to continue in good standing in his family relationships.

Dr. Helmer Mykelbust, in research at Northwestern University, points out that deafness affects the whole organism. He claims that not only is hearing affected, but vision, balance, taste, smell, maturation, and educational development are all altered because of a hearing problem. And, even further, Mykelbust states that it causes differences in perception. Knowing these things from research, one cannot say that this child with hearing problems should be treated the same as a hearing child. It is a disservice to the child to do so. This does not mean the deaf child should be set apart as peculiar, but is recognizing his problem for what it is.

What, then, are some suggestions that can help parents enjoy a better relationship with their hearing-handicapped children?

1. Tender, loving care is essential. Love and affection go far in cementing a bond of family unity. Dr. M. C. Hill says, "The vitamin of love is the greatest single thing we can give our children. Those who were blessed with the vitamin of love when they were young will mature into well-adjusted adults."

2. Children need to be spoken with, but parents must remember to adjust their speech to the vocabulary level of their child's speechreading. Parents should visit with their children patiently so that he really knows and understands not only what they are saying, but the "how and why" as well. Time should be taken for casual, and necessary conversation.

3. What parents demand of their children should be clear. Hearing children require much repetition for learning and the hearing-handicapped child needs much repetition, too. Because hearing handicapped children must be spoken to directly it will seem that the repetition is more excessive than it is to hearing children. Also, the

hearing-handicapped child can understand what is wanted more clearly if time is taken to *show* him.

4. The maturation rate of children should not be compared. Research shows that lack of hearing tends to slow down maturation, so the child who does not hear should not be expected to mature as rapidly as his hearing brothers and sisters.

5. Unless the hearing handicapped child is unusually bright, there will be an educational lag. Some authorities say there is a gap of three to seven years between hearing and deaf children. Parents should be cognizant of this fact and realize that there will be differences in the school situation.

6. The deaf child also tends to be slower in social development. Schools are making every effort to help the child by providing social situations for the children's development. This is an area where the home can provide many possibilities for growth.

7. The child should be made aware of his responsibilities as an integral part of the family and his home. He should not be the privileged weekend, month-end or vacation guest. Chores and privileges commensurate with his age and abilities are an important part of the building of a feeling of belonging to the family group.

8. The child's interests should be noticed. The child should be admired, and parents should take time to learn something their child wants to show them whether great or small.

9. Meals and bedtime are times for family closeness and pleasure.

10. Religious training should be started early. It may be a difficult area of understanding, but simple understanding is possible and necessary for the nurture of the child.

11. Parents should show that they are a source of strength.

12. Patience, friendliness, politeness and consideration of each other are family virtues which make parent-child relationships satisfactory to all. Consciousness of these traits should be uppermost in families with a hearing

handicapped child.

In conclusion, it should be remembered that the *deaf child should not be treated like any other child*, but rather, he should be treated with an understanding of his deafness. This new concept which requires compensation and education on the part of the parent is well worth the effort. Like all worthwhile endeavors, rearing a hearing handicapped child has its challenges, and it also has many satisfactions. All the joys of parenthood can be realized if the parental outlook consists of a realistic understanding of the organism, which is the child with a hearing handicap.

News Media Aid Schools

Traveling around the United States convinces one that the general public is ignorant of deafness and the residential school for the deaf. The public is still in the dark about the many changes which have taken place and are still taking place in residential schools. Technological and curricular changes are especially noticeable in this group. Many people are shocked to see that our students are using the same textbooks and following practically the same curricula as those used in public schools. Many people do not know that practically all of the residential schools are either state owned or state subsidized. The residential schools are not doing enough to publicize the work which is being done inside their doors. This failure to publicize the work is doing much harm to children that should be in the residential school and hurting the schools themselves.

Two specific instances show the need of better public relations! A distraught mother began asking questions about deafness. Upon close examination she admitted that she had a young deaf child. Further discussion brought out the fact that she and her husband were living in separate cities—the husband to hold onto an excellent position which he had worked hard to get; the wife to raise four children and to keep the deaf child living at home and in a public day school. Asked why the child was not sent to the state school the mother's answer was that the child would learn sign language. This mother had no idea of what went on at the state school. Through gossip she heard that residential schools do not teach speech. She accepted this gossip without checking further.

The other incident was a discussion held with a medical doctor. He had a child patient with a speech and hearing defect. The parents of the child were too poor to afford private tutoring and did not know what to do. Although the state residential school was only a few miles (less than 25) from the doctor's home he had no idea of what was going on there. He was surprised to learn of the many free services which could be obtained at the school.

In Iowa the newspaper is one of the best and most effective means of telling the public about the school. The Council Bluffs *Nonpareil* maintains a tremendous interest in the school and sees to it that the public is informed of what is going on. It keeps people informed in the following ways:

1. Teen Topics—One of the seniors writes a weekly column for the paper—telling about school activities, dormitory life, students, parties, teachers and any other events that take place at the school. To reward the writer the newspaper pays the reporter for the column. This column improves public relations, and gives the student an outlet for his writing and stimulates good writing for the student and provides some spending money.

2. Student Spotlight—Along with other high school students outstanding students are interviewed and their pictures are taken. This column depicts the personal life, hopes and ambitions of the students. It also gives the public an insight into what the students are doing and what they are capable of accomplishing.

3. National Surveys—Many teen-age current events questions are being asked nationally. In making up its program the Nonpareil includes I.S.D. students in its regular survey.

4. Athletics—All football, basketball and track events are covered by Nonpareil reporters. In addition, interviews and photographs of sport highlights are published regularly.

5. The honor roll, program notices (such as commencement

and Christmas), parties and academic and vocational events are newspaper material.

The newspaper is only one medium of informing the public of what is going on inside the residential school. Other means which have not been exploited to the fullest include TV, radio, movies, magazines, pamphlets, demonstrations, open houses, and speeches to civic and other organizations.

One year the Iowa Board of Regents invited the leading statewide organizations to meet at the five different institutions under its control. This provided a tremendous amount of publicity for Iowa School for the Deaf.

Activities such as scouting and Y-Teens, in which students mix with hearing boys and girls also create much interest in the school and give the student a chance to make new friends among hearing people.

The above are only some of the ways in which the Iowa School for the Deaf is attempting to make the public aware of what is going on behind its doors. Everyone in deaf education should be striving to give the public a better understanding of the deaf and their capabilities. By working together and sharing ideas everyone stands to benefit—the child, the adult, the teachers, the employers and the public in general. Everyone in the profession should make a concerted effort to promote good public relations.

Hearing Impaired People Can Help Medical Research

Medical research in the study of deafness has been lagging behind other areas of medicine for many years because: (1) The middle and inner ear are very difficult to study. (2) Pathologists have had no reason to probe the ears of deaf people in determining the cause of death. (3) Funds for setting up centers for specific study of this problem have been lacking.

In an effort to help this program and make ears available for study, the American Laryngolical, Rhinological, and Otological Society, supported by the Deafness Research Foundation voted to establish Temporal Bone Banks.

These bone banks are established at strategically located

centers across the nation where research data is available to anyone needing it.

The foundation wants only the ears of those having any type of hearing impairment.

Specific instructions have been set up by the American Laryngolical, Rhinological and Otological Society for the donation of temporal bones.

Persons who wish to donate their inner ear structures must have a documented case of hearing impairment and must obtain consent from next of kin.

A form may be obtained from the American Academy of Opthomology and Otolaryngology in Rochester, Minnesota, or from the Deafness Research Foundation, 310 Lexington Avenue, New York, New York.

The form gives specific donation directions.

It is hoped that anyone with a hearing impairment will seriously consider what a great help their temporal bones may make to future generations. It is possible that this type of research may cut future hearing impairments. At this point those with a hearing impairment have everything to gain and nothing to lose by helping the temporal bone bank. Unless medical science can study the workings of the middle and inner ears more closely, very little can be done to help.

Here, then, lies the opportunity for hearing impaired people to contribute to a program where some answers to the riddle of deafness may be found.

Only those with impaired hearing can make contributions. It is hoped that these people will seriously consider permitting these bone banks to inherit their temporal bones. This is one donation which will cost nothing and pay very high returns to future generations.

Chapter VI

PSYCHOLOGICAL ASPECTS

TESTING INTELLIGENCE QUOTIENTS

T ESTING THE INTELLIGENCE of a deaf person is intriguing and mystifying. The proper avenues of approach to testing the deaf are still not solved. The deaf person lacks adequate verbal communication. Verbal communication is an important aspect of intelligence and its lack automatically nullifies any test in which verbal abilities are the key factors. Performance type tests have achieved partial success. Whether it is possible to measure intelligence by the use of a performance scale only is questionable.

> Psychological research of the deaf has been handicapped from the beginning by a number of serious lacks. (Trained workers, adequate psychological instruments, normative criteria of evaluation, and communication relations in depth between workers and deaf subject.) (Levine, 1963, pp. 496-512.)

Despite these handicaps, a number of psychological studies have been conducted through the years.

One of the first serious studies of the intelligence of the deaf was made by Greenberger (1889). He apparently stumbled on the idea of using something like a psychological test when confronted with the problem of eliminating the feebleminded among children applying for admission to a school for the deaf. In addition to the ordinary test for hearing, Greenberger stated that it was necessary to find out something about the student's mental faculties. In order to do so he used attractive picture books which were shown to the child as the examiner watched. If the child remained apathetic, it was a bad sign. If, however, the child was attracted by the books and maintained an interest in them for a period of time, it was an indication of fair mentality that could be improved by training. Greenberger also proposed a number test, since an entire lack of an idea of numbers was, in his estimation, a sure sign of great weakness in a child's mind. He also showed the child forms and colors. Blocks were placed before the child and the examiner watched how well the child could build with them. Modern mental tests make use of all the materials which Greenberger suggested—pictures, blocks, colors and forms. Neither a standard method of procedures, nor an evaluation of the child's responses in terms of the responses of other children was suggested by Greenberger, and so the essential elements of a standardized mental test were lacking.

Taylor (1898) reported on a spelling test given to 148 deaf pupils and a similar number of hearing pupils. The test was a free association test. The pupils were told to write as many words as possible in fifteen minutes. The average number of words written by the deaf was 151; by the hearing, 153. The average number of spelling mistakes by the deaf was 2.7; by the hearing, 4.3. Hence, Taylor concluded that the deaf were superior in spelling ability. At no time, however, did Taylor point out the types or length of the words attempted by the hearing or the deaf.

Mott (1899), in her research of a comparison of eight-year-olds, compared the deaf and the hearing in all respects in which data of normal children were available. She used physical, and psychological, tests. With reference to mental factors, she stated, memory and observation seemed the only mental powers capable of exact comparison between the two classes of children. In physical measurements, in athletic contest, and manual dexterity, she found the deaf to be as good as hearing children. In memory and observation tests she found the deaf markedly superior to the hearing. Some of these results are contrary to those of later work.

Although the first few early tests were not definitive, they stimulated further testing. A report by MacMillan and Bruner (1906) showed one of the initial studies in which so-called psychological tests were given to the deaf. The tests were not the intelligence tests now in common use, but the tests of single abilities which preceded the general intelligence tests of the Binet type. The tests were both physical and mental. They included hearing, visual acuity, height, weight, and head measurements. The examiners found the deaf on the average below the hearing in lung capacity. There was not much difference in the strength grip. In the cancellation of age tests the deaf were on the average from two to three years less mature than hearing children of the same age. In visual memory span for numbers the deaf were definitely below the hearing.

MacMillan and Bruner concluded that the inferiority of the deaf on the mental side meant no more than that the children were from three to four years less mature than the hearing children of similar age and that the date of maturity would be correspondingly delayed. They felt that the gap would be closed in the future.

New avenues of psychological testing began to open in the early 1900's when Pintner and Patterson came on the scene. The introduction of the Binet-Simon Scale for Measurement of Intelligence started a new chapter in psychological measurement and an all inclusive measure of general ability took the place of the single specific tests of very narrow psychological function. In the study of the deaf, the only thorough attempt to apply the Binet test was made by Pintner and Patterson, the first workers to apply a general intelligence test to the deaf. They used the Goddard revision of the Binet-Simon Scale which was in general use at that time. Attempting to apply the tests by the use of written language, Pintner and Patterson presented typed questions to the child, and requested him to answer in writing. This method was soon abandoned because it at once became apparent that many children did not understand the written questions, but appeared to understand the same questions when asked by means of the manual alphabet or sign language. Therefore, the examiners used any method, or any combinations of methods—speech, speechreading, writing, signs, or finger spelling, to put the questions across. Twenty-two children were examined but only eighteen cases yielded enough information to compute a tentative mental age. Only one child tested at age level. All others showed retardation. The average chronological age was 12.5 years; the average mental age, 7.9 years. The average mental retardation was 4.58 years. Many subtest items were found to be totally unsuited for the deaf. The language of some of the questions was too difficult. Pintner and Patterson concluded that the use of the Binet Scale with the deaf was totally unsuitable. They suggested that performance type scales might be more suitable, and taking their own suggestions seriously, immediately started work with performance tests which led utlimately to the Pintner-Patterson Performance Scale.

Since tests of learning ability may be considered a type of intelligence test, Pintner and Patterson worked with the well-known Digit-Symbol and Symbol-Digit Test before the introduction of the modern type group intelligence test. Tests of hearing ability measure the rapidity with which new associations are formed by repetition. The more rapidly the subject learns symbols for digits, the less frequently does he need to refer to the key and his speed or performance increases. Pintner and Patterson tested 992 deaf children with the Digit-Symbol and 1,049 with the Symbol-Digit Test. A study of the results showed that at no age did the deaf child equal the norms for hearing children. The deaf were two to three years retarded at those ages where the best comparisons could be made. The average retardation on the Digit-Symbol Test was found to be 3.75 years and on the Symbol-Digit Test, 2.9 years.

Pintner and Patterson came to the following conclusions concerning the testing of deaf subjects:

1. The average I. Q. of the deaf did not quite reach 90.

2. The age of onset of deafness seemed to make no difference in the intelligence of the child.

3. There seemed to be no difference, on the average, between the intelligence of the congenitally deaf and the adventitiously deaf.

4. Both the large surveys found the average intelligence of the manually taught pupils below the average of the other two groups.

5. The difference in intelligence between pupils taught by the oral and the combined method was not great.

6. The average intelligence of the deaf child taught in day schools was slightly higher than the deaf child attending residential schools.

7. The residential school had more dull and backward pupils and fewer bright ones.

8. As compared with the hearing child, the deaf child was

about ten points below in I.Q. on non-language and performance tests.

    9. There seemed to be a large reservoir of fine native ability among the deaf. They were possessed of sound intelligence upon which education could build.

A review by Newlee (1919) showed the results of the Symbol-Digit and Digit-Symbol Tests given to 85 deaf children in a Chicago day school. The children ranged in age from six to eighteen years. The results from the Newlee test showed that:

1. The learning ability was normally distributed among the 85 students examined.
2. There was very little difference among the series.
3. The results disagreed with Pintner. (Pintner and Patterson used 1,000 cases, while Newlee used only 85. This may be the cause of the discrepancy.)

Patterson (1930) gave the Goodenough Test to 466 pupils, ages 4.9 to 21. The subjects were taken at random from five different residential schools for the deaf. His results were as follows:

1. The curve of distribution did not follow the normal curve for hearing children. A greater number were clustered at the lower portion of the curve. There was a normal decline at the upper portion of the scale.
2. Thirty-three percent of the pupils tested appeared at the average level of intelligence, which compared with forty-nine per cent of the hearing children grouped at the same level.
3. There was a wide difference in the intelligence rating of the children from the various schools.
4. The average degree of retardation of the deaf was found to be 22 months.

It must be remembered that some of the causes of retardation could be delay in beginning education, suitable methods of instruction and inability of students to assimilate language readily.

MacKane (1933) sought to find the reasons for the discrepancy in different test scores and discovered the now familiar fact that the I.Q. of a given individual can vary with the tests.

Some deaf children may be less than a year retarded on a performance scale and yet be two years retarded on "non-performance type" tests. MacKane's findings served as the impetus for activity in test standardization.

In considering this problem, Helen Schick (1934) asked the following questions:

> Can the intelligence of the deaf, or speech defective child, be measured on a scale that makes it possible to compare with normal hearing children? This question is a vital one for educators of the deaf and many approaches to the problem have been made. If we define intelligence as the ability to think abstractedly, as the ability to manage ideas and symbols, we should probably never find an adequate measure for the deaf child, because any test of this type involves linguistic ability. Furthermore, all school grades and teachers estimates are weighted on the side of abstract intelligence. If, however, we define intelligence as the ability to use judgment and adjust to various situations presented by the environment, then a performance test should give us a measure of a kind of intelligence that is important in our practical work, and a measure not so affected by school training as our linguistic tests. (Schick, 1934, pp. 651-652)

At Central Institute, St. Louis, Missouri, Max F. Meyer and Helen Schick measured performance of the deaf by use of a lectometer, an instrument which requires the formation of a generalization of pattern reversal which could be applied throughout the test. There were essentially no differences between deaf and hearing and the quotient could be computed that correlated highly with standardized intelligence tests. Schick and Meyer measured the performance ability of preschool age children with the Randall's Island Performance Series and yielded an average I.Q. of 97. They also used a revised Drever-Collins Test and found an I.Q. range from 75 to 152, with a mean of 105. The time element was extended for all tests but all the other scoring procedures were the same. There were no norms used for comparison. Schick and Meyer recommended further research.

Bishop (1936) conducted a very extensive study in the St. Paul Public School system, St. Paul, Minnesota, to determine the level of mental development in classes for the deaf and hard-of-hearing. He used the Arthur Performance Scale. This scale was given to each of ninety children admitted to the special classes for the deaf and hard-of-hearing between January, 1929 and May, 1936. The results showed that the I.Q.'s ranged from 68 to 152. The median was 97, and the mean 97.16. The findings indicated a normal distribution with as nearly an unselected deaf group as one can find in the general population.

Bridgeman (1939) attempted to estimate the mental ability of 90 deaf children. Eighty-three were either educational failures or had serious disturbance conduct problems. The other seven were selected by the school as being normal or superior in intelligence, successful in school progress, and socially normal. Bridgeman used the Arthur Point Scale, The Ontario School Ability Test, the Stanford revision of the Binet Scale, the Healy Scale Information Test and the Randall's Island Test. The results were as follows:

1. The range of ability was very wide, considerably greater than that found in most hearing cases. On two of the Arthur tests, the successful children were better than the bright failures.

2. On four of the tests, the brighter failures had a better record than the successful children. And on the remaining two tests there were no appreciable differences.

Bridgeman concluded that, although the number of the sample was small, these tests cannot always serve to predict school ability. The non-verbal tests were devised to test other than academic capacities and their use with deaf children indicated that a certain number of children may have adequate ability along non-verbal lines, while academically they are seriously retarded. In spite of the non-verbal tests' failure to indicate educational success or failure in some instances, the tests serve apparently to rule out mentally inferior cases. For example, a child with an I.Q. below 80 will probably have difficulty with academic subjects.

Zekel and van der Kolk (1939) gave the Porteus Maze Test to 100 deaf and 120 hearing children. They found that the younger deaf were more inadequate than the older deaf but came to the conclusion that the deaf would catch up to the hearing as they grew older. Zekel and van der Kolk also found that the younger hearing were more inadequate than the older hearing, so it is difficult to understand what is meant by the improvement of the deaf as they grow older, because the hearing improved with age also. The average I.Q. for the deaf group was reported as 86.1, and for the hearing group as 99.4.

Kline (1945) investigated the responses of deaf children in a free association test and compared them to hearing children and hearing adults. Using deaf children ranging in age from 11 to 17, he checked the responses to printed stimulus words and compared them to hearing children of the same ages. The words were familiar to the deaf subjects. Kline reported that the responses of the deaf children to free association words were different from those of hearing children with more failures of response among the deaf, along with a larger percentage of very common responses. Personality content analysis was not conducted.

Birch and Birch (1951) conducted a research on a series of 53 deaf cases to whom the Leiter and two other intelligence tests had been administered. The tests, other than the Leiter, were among those often used with deaf children including the Arthur Point Scale Performance Tests, the Nebraska Test of Learning Aptitude for Young Deaf Children, The Performance Scale of Wechsler's Adult Intelligence Scale, Form I, and the Goodenough Draw A-Man Test.

Birch and Birch concluded that the Leiter Scale gives I.Q.'s which are consistently lower than those of other tests commonly used for the deaf. This seemed to be the most general, and most important conclusion, drawn from this study conducted at the Western Pennsylvania School for the Deaf.

Birch and Birch pointed out that it should be kept in mind that the sample in the study was made up almost entirely of children who had been educational problems in a school for the deaf in that they had been relatively unsuccessful in learning speechreading, speech, and reading. According to Birch and Birch, the nature of these cases may suggest an important way in which the Leiter Scale could be useful. It may be that when the Leiter score is considerably below the scores of the Arthur and the Nebraska, one can predict that the child will be a serious teaching problem in speechreading, speech and reading. Also, it may be that when both the Leiter and Goodenough scores are low, and the Nebraska and Arthur scores are high, the learning problems of the child will be even more serious. The reader must bear in mind that this is not an established fact, but rather, it is a possibility which needs further investigation.

The reasoning behind Birch and Birch's hypothesis was as follows: There is substantial evidence that the Stanford-Binet Revised Scale is a good predictor of academic aptitude, or school learning success. It is not perfect, but it is good. None of the tests commonly used for the deaf is known to have this characteristic of prediction. However, Arthur and Leiter have stated that they consider the Leiter Scale to be a nonverbal instrument which resembles the Stanford-Binet. This research is not substantiated by any statistical data and the conclusions are only those of Birch and Birch.

Larr and Cain (1959) attempted to support information which would verify the usefulness of the Wechsler Intelligence Scale for Children in measuring the abilities of the deaf. They used 248 subjects from a residential school for the deaf, ages 8 to 19, with a hearing loss exceeding 75 decibels, The Wechsler-Bellevue, Form II, was administered and the tests were given over a two year period. Additional tests administered to the group were the Arthur, the Ontario, the Nebraska, and the Goodenough. The results were as follows:

1. The Wechsler-Bellevue showed a range of I.Q.'s from 61 to 138, with a mean of 97.8.

2. The Arthur, on 77 pupils, showed a range of 61 to 147, with a mean of 101.1.

3. The Ontario, with 63 pupils, showed a range of 52 to 129, with a mean of 98.1.

Larr concluded that the WISC correlated with the Ontario to the extent of .786 on the Pearson r. He also found that the WISC and the Arthur correlated at .867 on the Pearson r. Larr makes no mention of the correlations with the Nebraska or the Goodenough Tests. His conclusions, however, were that the WISC is a useful tool for the assessment of nonverbal abilities of deaf children. Larr and Cain failed to point out that the WISC has no norms on deaf children.

Myklebust (1958) stated that it is becoming clear that deaf children should not be considered inferior in intelligence, as compared to the general population. He pointed out that the use of the qualitative aspects of their perceptual and conceptual functioning and their reasoning, does seem to be different. More research evidence would be helpful in clarifying the nature of the intellectual capacities of children who have sustained deafness in early life. Currently, it can be stated that it is difficult for the deaf to live up to the potential of their intellectual capacity. It is difficult for them to use their intelligence in a manner that is as broad, as subtle and as abstract as that of the hearing. Myklebust administered the Wechsler-Bellevue Intelligence Test to deaf children. Using 85 subjects, ages 12 to 17, he derived a mean of 66.5 on the verbal scores. On performance scale, the same group had a mean quotient of 101.8. Myklebust pointed out that the verbal scores were derived from five sub-tests of the performance part.

Stunkel (1957) studied the intelligence of deaf and hearing college students on the verbal and non-verbal portions of Federal Service Entrance Examinations. The deaf students selected were practically all from Gallaudet College, Washington, D. C. The study showed that deaf people demonstrated above-average ability on non-verbal reasoning tests and a marked weakness in all the tests of verbal nature included in the study. Stunkel submitted the view that the deaf function differently from the hearing.

The reviews of the psychological studies presented in this part of the section have outlined the major efforts in the field up to the present time with the exception of research done in relation to the Nebraska Test of Learning Aptitude.

The psychological testing done with the deaf has been sparse, sketchy and essentially initial in scope.

CATEGORIES OF PSYCHOLOGICAL TESTING

Education of the deaf tends to fall in two categories concerning psychological testing of the deaf. First, some educators feel that deaf children should be compared with hearing children since the ultimate aim is to fit deaf children into a hearing environment. Second, other educators of the deaf express the idea that it is not how the deaf child ranks with the hearing, but how he ranks in comparison with other deaf children. Earlier in this section attention was given to research studies which compared the intelligence of the deaf child with the intelligence of the hearing child. In most instances the testing instruments used were those which had been developed for the hearing. Conclusions reached on the studies were based on instruments developed for hearing children. The question now arises, were these instruments valid? Can one judge a deaf person by hearing standards? Is it possible for one to use an instrument standardized on the hearing to draw conclusions for the deaf?

Hiskey pondered these questions and concluded that the psychological instruments developed for the hearing could not be used adequately for the assessment of the deaf. Hiskey (1941) hypothesized that the deaf should be compared to other deaf in psychological assessment. Seeing the need for this type of instrument, Hiskey developed the Nebraska Test of Learning for Young Deaf Children, one of the few tests in the world which has been standardized on the deaf.

The Nebraska Test of Learning Aptitude for Young Deaf Children is a performance type of test consisting of eleven subtests in which speed is eliminated. All items were chosen with special reference to the limitations of the deaf with the final item selection based chiefly upon the criterion of age differentiation. Norms were based on 466 children, ages four through ten years, who were attending state schools for the deaf in seven states.

The Nebraska Test of Learning Aptitude Manual gives the following data on Hiskey's test.

In the selection and construction of test items, every item of the scale was considered in light of the following criteria:

1. Was the item similar to the task or tasks which the young deaf child did in school?
2. Was it the type which could be included in a non-verbal test?

3. Could the items be presented in such a way that directions could be given through simple pantomine?
4. Was it the type of item which experience had shown to yield high correlation with acceptable criteria of intelligence or learning ability?
5. Could the item be constructed and presented in such a way that the child could make a definite response, thus making the scoring objective and easily done?
6. Would the item be appealing or attractive to the subject?
7. Could the item be scored without the score being based on time?
8. Did the difficulty of the item appear to be within the age range of the standardizing group?
9. Did the item seem likely to show discriminative capacity?

Since test items which were of the speed or time type were not to be used, it was decided to use groups of items of the same type arranged in order of difficulty. Thus, each group of items became a small power test in itself. In many instances, in order to meet all the above criteria, it was necessary to devise special methods of constructing or assembling the parts of an item. All the items are of a type which had been used before, but few of them had ever been assembled or used in the manner which they are in the present scale. The preliminary scale was composed of eighteen different types of items with a total of 204 parts.

In order to test the scale, it was given a preliminary trial. The primary purpose of such a trial was the elimination of the least satisfactory items and to help arrange the items in each group in order of their difficulty.

The preliminary trial provided helpful data for the selection of arrangement of tests. Those items which appeared to function the most satisfactorily and to most nearly approximate the criteria were retained. The criteria were the following:

1. Validity based on the per cents passing from one age to the next.
2. Ease of administering.
3. Ease and objectivity of scoring.
4. Attractiveness or interest to the subject.

5. Variety.

6. Time of administering.

When the sifting process was completed eleven types of tests were retained, including a total of 124 individual parts.

Perhaps the most common method of interpreting scores had been the familiar Binet type mental age. Age norms were used and the amount of mental development in a year was the unit of measurement. Age norms were established for raw scores and were converted into, or interpreted as mental ages. This age-type score representing the amount of development up to date, has much greater meaning to the layman than does the standard score or the percentile score and for that reason the age norm has been used in this scale. However, the term *mental age* has not been used because the mental age would undoubtedly suggest a Binet mental age which in turn would suggest a corresponding mental age of the hearing child, and thus lead to false comparisons. For this reason and the fact that the test items had been selected, in many instances, because of the similarity to the abilities which the deaf child must exhibit in school, the term *learning age* was used instead.

A learning age of 5-0 means that according to the results of this test, the child is able to do those tasks which the average deaf child of five years is able to do, or, that he should be able to solve problems with the same average efficiency as the average deaf five-year-old. One can easily see that the Hiskey Nebraska Test was standardized and developed for the deaf to be used as a comparison to the deaf.

The Hiskey Test has been introduced in many schools for the deaf. Investigation has been made to obtain more information concerning the reliability and validity of the test, to compare hearing and deaf children on this scale, and to analyze the test items in terms of the increasing difficulty as related to increased chronological age and compare the order of difficulty of the test items for hearing and deaf subjects.

Land and McPherson (1948) found the following results: (1) The Nebraska Test of Learning Aptitude is a valid test of intelligence. (2) Correlated with performance scales—.74 for the deaf, and .90 for the hearing. (3) Additional evidence is that

54.3 per cent of the learning test scores vary less than ten points from the scores on the performance test.

The investigation showed the Hiskey Test to be a valid measure of mental ability and reliable for use in re-tests. The increasing difficulty for each six-month interval of chronological age was computed for the learning test. The gain in months of learning age from one interval to the next was not consistent. At some intervals the gain in months of learning age was far greater than the gain in months of chronological age, and at other intervals, the reverse was true. Perhaps this spotted gain and loss of months of learning age can be attributed to one, or both, of the following factors: (1) technical faults in the construction of the test, making it too easy at some levels, and too difficult at others, or (2) differences in the educational opportunities of the groups tested.

The original Hiskey Test seems to be heavily weighted in visual memory, since five of the eleven sub-tests involve this mental faculty. The hearing handicap of the deaf entails an emphasis upon visual education and visual aids to learning, and it is possible that the visual weighting of the learning test has given the deaf an advantage over the hearing.

In reviewing the Hiskey Test for Buros, Mildred Templin (1951) characterized the Hiskey Test as follows:

This test is constructed specifically for young deaf and hard-of-hearing children and has been standardized on such a group.

Hiskey's contribution to the psychological testing for the deaf has been of immeasurable value. The use of this test has become continually more widespread, in fact, worldwide in its scope. He has completed a revision of his Nebraska Test of Learning Aptitude (1964) which should further enhance his contribution.

The ability to forecast school achievement in deaf children would be of acknowledged value. To date researchers have had little success in finding a way to make valid predictions. Previous research studies on the original Hiskey-Nebraska Test of Learning Aptitude were usually of a comparative type in that the Hiskey-Nebraska Test of Learning Aptitude was compared to other intelligence instruments. Research has not shown the relationship between learning age as determined by the Hiskey Scale and academic gains as measured by an achievement scale as a basis of prediction. Any information regarding the possible prediction of school achievement would be beneficial to the entire deaf educational profession.

The purpose of Giangreco's (1965) research was to explore the relationship between the learning age obtained in the revised Hiskey-Nebraska Test of Learning Aptitude and several achievement scales to determine whether the Hiskey-Nebraska Test of Learning Aptitude (Revised) could be used as a predictor of academic achievement for deaf children.

Subjects for the research were 235 deaf students ranging in age from 7-17, in residence at the Iowa School for the Deaf. All of the students were given the Hiskey-Nebraska Test of Learning Aptitude (Revised) as well as the Stanford Achievement Test, The Gates Reading Test, The Metropolitan Achievement Test and a Teacher Rating Scale by Giangreco.

The Pearson r was the statistical instrument used to measure the correlations between the Hiskey-Nebraska Test of Learning Aptitude (Revised) and the achievement ratings. Computers at the University of Nebraska were used for the actual computation. The Fischer Table was used to determine the level of confidence. The students were broken up in seven separate groups—by age and class. Appropriate forms of the achievement test were given to each group level.

The results were as follows:

GROUP I (20 students. Age range 7-1 to 8-6)
A significant relationship was found at the .05 level for all the subtests on the Gates, The Metropolitan and Teacher Rating Scale.

GROUP II (43 students. Age range 8-1 to 10-7)
The subjects had been in school three to four years. There was significant relationship at the .05 level with all the achievement test subscores, on the Gates, Metropolitan and The Teacher Rating Scale.

GROUP III (26 students. Age range 10-1 to 12-0. Fifth year classes)

Correlations at this level were not significant at the .05 or .10 level. Correlations ranged from .052 (Arithmetic Computation) to .215 (Arithmetic Reasoning) on the Stanford. Correlations on the Gates and Metropolitan were very low. There were even some minus correlations. Correlations of the Teacher Rating Scale were not significant.

GROUP IV (26 students. Age range 11-3 to 13-8. Sixth and seventh-year classes)

All of the subtests were significant at the .05 level on the Stanford. With the exception of Word Knowledge and Word Discrimination all of the subtests on the Metropolitan were significant. All of the subtests on the Gates were significant at the .05 level. The subtests on the Teacher Rating Scale were significant for attention span, recall and common sense.

GROUP V (32 students. Age range 13-1 to 14-9. Eighth year classes)

With the exception of Arithmetic Computation, all of the subtest scores on the Stanford lacked significance at the .05 level. On the Metropolitan, Word Knowledge, Word Discrimination, Reading and Language the results were not significant, however, the Arithmetic Computation and Reasoning results were significant. All of the Gates subtests and The Teacher Rating subtests results were not significant.

GROUP VI (36 students. Age range 14-0 to 16-9. Freshman and sophomore classes)

On the Stanford correlations for Paragraph Meaning, Word Meaning, Spelling, Social Studies and Science were not significant at the .05 level; Language, Arithmetic Computation and Problem Solving, Study Skills were significant at the .05 level.

The Metropolitan subtest scores indicated that correlations for Word Knowledge, Spelling, Social Studies Information, Social Studies Skills and Science were not significant. Correlations for Reading, Language, Language Study Skills,

Arithmetic Computation and Arithmetic Problem Solving, were significant.

The correlations for each of the subtests on the Gates Reading Test were significant at the .10 level. The correlations on The Teacher Rating Scale were not significant at the .05 level.

GROUP VII (25 students. Age range 15-0 to 17-2. Junior and senior high school classes)
All of the achievement tests and The Teacher Rating Scale were significant at the .05 level.

Arithmetic Computation and Arithmetic Reasoning showed the highest as well as the most consistent correlations throughout the entire sample. Low correlations were found mostly in subject matter requiring reading skill such as English, literature, composition, science, and social studies.

A "gray area" stood out distinctly at the fifth, sixth, seventh and ninth year levels. Practically all of the correlations at the fifth, sixth, seventh, and ninth year levels were not significant at the .05 level. Significant and high correlations were found in low elementary years and in the advanced high school years. Scores obtained on The Teacher Rating Scale were consistent with correlations obtained on subtest scores on the achievement scales.

There was very little difference between the Stanford and Metropolitan correlations.

The entire study presented an interesting picture. The correlations tended to be significant at the lower and higher ends of the scale. This may make it possible to predict achievement at these levels through the use of the Hiskey-Nebraska Test of Learning Aptitude (Revised). In the middle years the opposite appears to be true. The cause of failure at this level has not been determined. Several possibilities come to the foreground for consideration which should perhaps be studied in depth.

1. The learning age seems to show consistent growth throughout the child's school career.

2. It may be that the achievement tests are not adequate for

the upper elementary years and that a new instrument is needed.

3. It is a time of adjustment for the children. They change dormitories, school buildings, and curricula, and the period of adolescence begins. It may be that this might affect the learning process.
4. It also may be that the child reaches a point where he must catch up at this level and it takes longer to grasp material.
5. Finally, the material changes from a concrete to an abstract nature. This causes a great deal of difficulty.

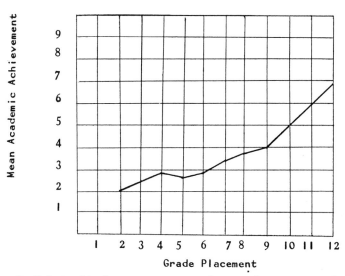

CHART 1: Relationship between mean academic achievement and grade level.

From the results of the Giangreco study it can be concluded that it may be possible to predict academic achievement by the use of the learning age scale of the Hiskey-Nebraska Test of Learning Aptitude (Revised) at the elementary and high school levels. The results suggest areas for further study. Additional research might be conducted using another intelligence test to check correlations with the same achievement tests used by Giangreco. The upper elementary level should be segregated for

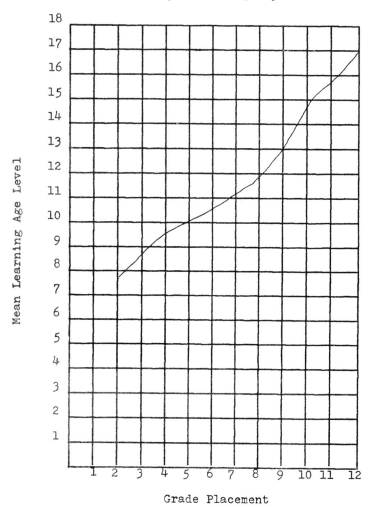

CHART 2: Relationship between mean learning and age level and grade placement.

more thorough study, considering the type of subjects the students study in relationship to the breakdown in these grades. There is a possibility that such a study would necessitate the development of special measuring techniques. Noting the personal and social problems of this group, perhaps the non-school hours should be observed more closely to discern the relationship of non-school activities to the problem.

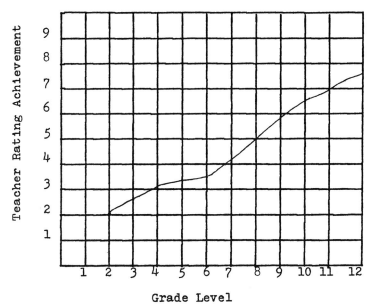

Grade Level

CHART 3: Relationship between mean teacher rating achievement and grade level.

The results of Giangreco's research should be an incentive for future study so that some of the learning problems which are now affecting the education of the deaf may be investigated and eventually alleviated. Many problems have been faced in an attempt to give the deaf the best possible tools for living. The hearing handicapped not only have medical and electronic help, but also have psychological help which strives to enlighten even further problems confronting the hearing impaired segment of our society. More and more the hearing handicapped are being considered individuals with uniquenesses all their own that need careful study if further strides forward are to be taken to enhance their place in the world.

Chapter VII

PROFESSIONAL HINTS

PRINCIPALS AND SUPERVISING TEACHERS

T HE FOLLOWING is a speech given at the Convention of American Instructors of the Deaf at the Colorado School for the Deaf, Colorado Springs, Colorado.

Today I have been entrusted with the responsibility of discussing with you some of the problems facing principals and supervising teachers. We all have varied reasons for being in these positions and have no doubt arrived at these stations by a variety of paths. How we got here is unimportant. What is important is, "Why are we here?" Why do schools for the deaf, or any other schools for that matter, have people in supervisory positions? First of all, we must recognize that when a school has more than one teacher, there is a division of responsibility and as staffs increase in number, the division of work gets more and more complicated. This is when it becomes necessary for some one to be able to look over the whole situation and decide where we are going and how are we going to get there. Hence, administration. Coordination of departments classification of students, curriculum choices, extracurricular activities, school-home relationships, medical services, and all other facets of developing children into adults must be given consideration. To be able to give proper decisions regarding all these avenues of growth, it is all important to keep in mind just what the principles that guide us are. These have been set up by the National Education Association as the seven cardinal principles of education and they apply to us as well as to the public schools. Everything that is done in a school should fit under one of these principles and should further the pupil's growth in one of these areas. If it does not, it should be eliminated. If there is not proper balance of these principles, balance should be sought.

The seven cardinal principles are as follows:

Health

Social, as well as personal efficiency, depends upon health. The school can teach facts about health, help pupils form good

150

health habits, and build attitudes which will promote health. The aim should not be attacked as an isolated unit or as an abstraction, but in relation to other aims and through the medium of all subjects of the curriculum. The health services of the school, the dormitory attitude, and any other campus influences are equally important with actual direct and indirect teaching in the classroom.

Command of the fundamental process

This is probably the best known of the seven principles and generally refers to basic skills in reading, writing, and arithmetic. Proficiency should be acquired and retained by suitable exercises. Deficiencies should be noted and remedial treatment given. Naturally, skills should be increased in a continuing manner throughout the school years.

Worthy home membership

An understanding of the importance of the home as a social institution and one's place and duties in it is embodied in the aim of the worthy home membership. This aim should be taught incidentally. However, the outcomes should be primary. Teaching one in school to be a better member of a home involves a transfer of training, for one cannot make the school like home. It is not even desirable to do so. School life is as worthy as home life, and one learns to be a member of one through participation in the other because of common elements between them.

Vocational efficiency

Everyone at some time in life is responsible for his own welfare and usually for that of others. This means that each person in society should gain proficiency as a social aim. It became an educational aim when it was accepted by the schools, for they felt that they could make a good contribution to vocational training. The multitude of different occupations, the period of training required for them and the changing society which requires adaptation have caused more emphasis to be placed on vocational training. The increase in school population and the urbanization of the population have caused a demand for graduates who are more specifically prepared for a vocation. This aim can be overemphasized, for too much time can be devoted to vocational work, at the neglect of other aims. Vocational work in schools should be aimed at giving a basis for vocational work, rather than extensive training in specific fields. The fundamentals of arithmetic and English, health and ethical character, are basic to any vocation. Because of limited time and facilities, the large task of the school should not be the development of a specific vocational training to a point of high degree proficiency. To desire a high degree of proficiency would force the selection of a vocation at an early age, without sufficient time to explore aptitudes. To expect a pupil to choose a lifetime work when he can't decide what to put on to wear to school every morning is ridiculous. Furthermore, one cannot predict accurately what vocational training is most needed because of the changing economic world. Therefore, the chief function of this fundamental principle is to help each pupil explore his own aptitudes, become acquainted with the world of work so he can make a wise vocational choice, and have sufficient background to begin pursuing it.

Citizenship

The committee which formulated the cardinal principles made the following comment concerning civic education: Civic education should develop in the individual those qualities whereby the individual will act well his part as a member of neighborhood, town, city, state, and nation, and give him a basis for understanding international problems.

For such citizenship, the following are essential: A many-sided interest in the welfare of the communities to which one belongs; loyalty to ideals of civic righteousness; practical knowledge of social agencies and institutions; good judgment as to means and methods that will promote one social end without defeating others; and as putting all these in effect, habits of cordial cooperation in social undertakings. All school subjects and all aims help foster good citizenship.

Worthy use of leisure

Increasingly, training in the worthy use of leisure is becoming more important. The working day is shorter. Child labor is virtually nonexistent and with the urbanization of the population, household and/or family chores are greatly diminished. Therefore, the selection of leisure-time activities is important. And, with the increase of commercialized amusements, it requires careful scrutiny to choose desirable ways to spend time. The school has the task of teaching pupils in one situation and how to fill their leisure hours in another. Leisure activities should be recreational, healthful, and, if possible, educational. Pupils should be taught to utilize the common means at their disposal in their own homes and communities for leisure pursuits, as found in sports, games, literature, art, music, and science. School activities should be selected with this idea in mind.

Ethical Character

Crime and delinquency have revealed that youth who are incapable of directing their own conducts are a menace to society. Ethical character should be taught indirectly, but every facet of the school program should make a contribution to it. It is comparable to good sportsmanship and fair play in athletics; honesty in all school work; respect for property, law, order, and authority; and attitude of reverence for a supreme being.

These seven points are our aims for building our school policy. Some are directly taught in the classroom. Most of them are the responsibility of every person on campus. The whole school must work toward their fulfillment. The administrators of a school have the job of seeing to it that this is done. Administrators must be aware of the distinction between ideal objectives and activity objectives. For example, good citizenship may be analyzed into the ideal of a good citizen and the activities of a good citizen. It is the latter with which one deals in selecting the activities to meet the objectives. The difference is similar to that of a definition and a description. A definition of an ideal citizen might furnish one a goal or standard toward which to work, but the description would involve an analysis of his activities, duty and responsibilities. The latter only can furnish a working basis for building a school curriculum to achieve the objectives.

The principles just reviewed deal with the development of the whole child through the entire school program. Now, let us turn our thoughts more specifically to the curriculum of the academic schoolday. This presents many age-old questions: What shall we teach? How shall we teach? Can we all have accredited high schools? How long shall periods be? What about records?

Before discussing this topic, I think it might be a good idea to first discuss deafness as an educational handicap. Many times we forget what this implies. I feel that we get so close to our school work that we are not aware of realistic facts.

This past winter, I was jolted into reality as I watched my six-year-old daughter progress through the first grade. She did not attend kindergarten. She is average in her ability. In the following paragraphs I will summarize her accomplishments in her first year of school and follow it with a summary of the first year of a deaf student.

Marianne loves to read. She completed the three preprimers and primer books 1 and 2 of the Scott-Foresman series plus thirty outside reading books. Workbooks completed include the *Think and Do workbooks* that accompany the Scott-Foresman Readers. She also completed a phonics workbook and knows all the sounds orally and written. She can sound out new words fairly well and uses context and pictures to the utmost in reading.

Writing has been a source of grumbling. Marianne prints manuscript style. Due to poor coordination and late muscle development, she started out very poorly, but has achieved moderately neat expression.

Formal spelling began with the second semester with five words a week being required learning. At first it was a week's work to learn to write the words correctly, but by the end of the year it was a simple two-day job to have them mastered. She received perfect Friday tests except for three. Personally, she had no opinion of like or dislike for the subject. She has also learned to spell words from sounding out and using known words. For example, knows *red* can spell *bed*.

Marianne enjoys English. She has good oral usage and is able to relate an incident or information with ease and interest. She accepts criticism and tries to improve diction and usage always. She recognizes proper written forms for "is and are," "have and has," "come and came," and others.

Arithmetic was totally distasteful. It was a struggle from the start, but in spite of this she has learned to count to 100 and can add and subtract combinations to 10. She has a fair understanding of money.

Art began poorly, but has improved throughout the year, but is still below average. She knows all colors and enjoys using them, however.

Science was sheer delight to Marianne. She did excellent work in it and learned general information about the universe (stars, sun, earth, etc.), weather (clouds, rain, snow, hot, cold, etc.), animals (names of wild and domesticated, life cycles of some), plants (life cycles and how seeds travel), names of some food (names of health needs), health (sleep, eat, exercise, teeth, brushing, cleanliness, etc.).

Marianne also had much to learn about being in social situations during her first year in school.

Now, let us look at what the deaf child completes in his first year of school.

Speechwise, he learns to use simple words and phrases. In speechreading, he is able to handle speech words and phrases and some sentences. Number work consists of learning to count to 10.

There is no formal reading. Some art and physical education are participated in. For the most part, however, the first year is primarily one of social adjustment.

These are the facts. A hearing child learns. A deaf child learns. Each spends the same time in school—180 days. Can we expect them to complete their formal public education at the same level of achievement? Can the ratio be changed? Should it be changed?

I feel that we must have a three- four- or even five-tract curriculum to take care of as many individual needs of the children as possible. Close study, observation, and testing should be started early to determine the learning capacities of the different students. At the Iowa School we have been running a four tract curriculum. So far, it seems satisfactory, but it will need constant care and supervision.

Too many of our students are being forced to sit through classes which are not at their educational level. This hurts any child.

A close check should be made on the time allotted for different subjects to see whether there is a balance or duplication, or even a waste of time in certain subjects.

We discussed vocational objectives earlier, but at this time, let me add a few more remarks. Criticism is being leveled at some residential schools over the fact that some authorities feel that too much time is being spent in vocational departments in proportion to academic time. Maybe it would be a good idea for all of us to check our vocational departments to find out whether or not some of this time can be used more advantageously elsewhere. Today with the blossoming of state departments of vocational rehabilitation, it might prove to be that our schools and their services can work more closely together so that there will be a common goal without duplicating services. The language arts present a real challenge. It might be that by giving two or three times more English to the deaf student as the hearing child receives, that part of the educational gap can be closed. In Iowa we have been giving a double period in English, but beginning next fall, we plan to give a triple period. It will be interesting to see what the end result will be in our middle and upper areas.

Regardless of the outcome, we should never give up hope and we must continuously strive to inspire the quality of education which is being given at our schools. Administrators should visit other schools, study the latest methods and not be afraid to make changes. A progressive school makes changes all the time.

What takes place after school hours is vitally important to the welfare of the classroom. Often we can sum this up by saying as the dormitories go, so goes the school. When things don't go right in the dorm, a child reflects his upset feeling in the tone and caliber of his studies. If anything is accomplished in such situations, it is never of the highest caliber that the particular student can do.

What is the solution to this problem of dormitory influence? Probably the first thing that comes to mind is the fact that too many counselors or house parents are not qualified to do the work they are doing. In most schools the pay is poor and the hours are miserable so that capable people are not attracted to these jobs. The people that do accept them do not understand the great responsibility which is theirs. For that reason, the dormitories do not contribute as much as they should to the total school program.

In Iowa we have tried to meet this problem by bringing in college trained people to be counselors who also are part-time teachers. The men which we have hired have backgrounds in recreation and education. Some are used in the vocational shops and some are in the academic classrooms. The salary of a 40 hour week counselor and the salary of a part-time teacher combine to make an attractive paycheck to qualified personnel. Besides the satisfactory paycheck, we have also been able to arrange schedules so that there is no split shift. These combination staff members begin work at 1:15 and stay on the job until all the children are in bed. Teachers who live in at the school have also cooperated in the counseling program and work during odd hours in the dormitory. They are happy to be in the dormitories for an hour or two in the mornings, and it has no ill effect on their teaching or morale. During weekends, students from the University of Omaha are eager for work and are good assistants in the dormitory. Although this probably sounds like a complicated system, it is working out very well and the students seem to be happy and well-satisfied with the arrangement. In fact, there has been an influx of new ideas in activities for out-of-school hours since we have been under this system and the students are exposed to an unusually wide variety of constructive leisure time activity, resulting in less sub-standard actions on the part of the students.

Working with the counselors during after school recreation hours, there are additional recreation workers who plan and help the counselors carry out their program. Balancing the dormitory life with a sound recreation program has been beneficial to everyone and we hope we are on the right track.

This program which I have discussed is only experimental and will require close watching. The results so far, however, are encouraging and should improve as the entire school becomes more familiar and proves itself acceptable.

The work of the counselors must never be underestimated. They should be told how important they are and how their work influences the work of all the school. Taking counselors into confidence will pay off in the long run. Never forget that they are closer to the children than any other people on the campus. They are a very important arm of the educational program.

The administrators of the school have tremendous responsibilities on their shoulders when it is realized that the success or failure of a school lies directly in their hands. It is no easy task to mesh the seven cardinal principles into a working arrangement that is forward moving and satisfying to all persons involved. The person in charge must lead the way through inspiration, planning, foresight, and creativity. In order to be this kind of person, certain characteristics are invaluable. If they are not a part of your present personality, you should make a concentrated effort of cultivating them.

Courage is necessary, as there are innumerable problems that must be faced with unwavering firmness. There are times when the chips must simply fall where they may.

A leader should not ask others to do anything which he himself would not do. The trend is for teachers to go to schood periodically to "keep fresh and abreast with current changes." The administrator must be willing to lead the way in order to show that this is really a worthwhile thing to do for the betterment of the school and the individual himself.

It is necessary to be ambitious and industrious. A person in a supervisory capacity must be willing to work, work, work. A person given administrative duties must recognize the fact that he is not on the same level as teachers. He is being paid more salary to do more work. It amuses me to hear the poor overworked supervising teacher or principal tell how he doesn't have time to do the many things which are required of him. Invariably, it is this same person, however, who leads the pack out of a school when the last class whistle blows. Paperwork that the principal or supervising teacher must do should be done after regular school hours. Schooltime is a time for supervision of classrooms. An administrator must be able to understand other people. He must be honest and objective with dealings involving teachers and students. The mind must be open at all times, and there should be no room for prejudices and favoritism.

A school is only as good as its leaders. Weak leadership will produce a weak school. Strong leadership will produce a strong school. Teachers and students are very sensitive about leadership and usualy play the old game of follow the leader. Therefore, the ability to inspire is uppermost. Inspiration can often be the difference between work that is passable and work that is above average.

The ability to accept criticism is not always one of the more gracious traits. Too many people feel that when they get in the position of being a leader, they are "untouchable." Never forget that all of us are human and are very capable of making mistakes. Administrators should be open to any criticism—constructive and destructive—and be glad to get it.

The principal or supervising teacher is entrusted with much power. It should be used discreetly. His integrity should be beyond reproach.

In conclusion, principals and supervising teachers must never let down their guard. They must never let themselves get stale or fall into the well-worn rut. Too much responsibility rests on the administrator's shoulders. It is necessary to hold up the trust that is placed in us by showing that we are truly leaders.

PARENTAL COUNSELING—A MUST

Probably one of the biggest problems facing administrators of schools for the deaf is that of parent counseling. Administrators must work with parents, and counseling them presents many difficult problems. Those in the field of administration should begin to take the time to see what can be done to help parents understand their children, understand the school, and understand themselves.

The following are some of the major problems with which parents of deaf children are confronted:

1. The parent has a difficult time understanding the educational implications of deafness. This includes the fields of reading, writing, mathematics, speech, and speechreading. Too many parents believe that a school for the deaf has a magical formula to produce speech and speechreading geniuses—students who can learn on par with hearing children and students who have the same social standing as the hearing child.

2. Parents are confused by the terminology used by educators of the deaf. There seems to be a difference of opinion among medical schools, educators, and laymen as to what deafness really is.

3. There is much confusion as to how much a deaf child can learn. Different people tell a parent different things. The result is confusing.

4. Schools for the deaf differ in regard to grade classifica-

tion, grades, and number of years in school. There are no set standards. Too many descriptions are used loosely; for example, the child may be in third grade while he is barely doing work at the first grade level.

5. There is much confusion in regard to grade status in the same grade level. For example, in most schools an "A" class is the best, and students in the class are usually doing different work than the "C" or "D" classes at the same grade level. Parents want an explanation of this.

6. The problem of the multiple handicapped child is one of grave concern. Parents want this child educated the same as other deaf children. In many states there are no facilities for this type of child. The result is that an increasing number enter schools for the deaf. In too many instances schools are not equipped to cope with these problems, yet parents and state officials demand that something be done.

7. Social adjustment is another big problem facing parents. Many parents feel that the deaf child does not belong when he gets home; he does not fit in with his peers. There seems to be a great deal of frustration between parents and child, and the family comes back to the school for help.

What can be done to help the parents understand their child in regard to school and home? Although the Iowa School for the Deaf still has a long way to go, it has begun an intensive program to bring the parents into focus and try to help answer the many frustrating questions which confront them.

Probably one of the most important steps was taken when a parent visitation program was inaugurated. Basically, in this program all the parents were invited to come to the school as guests. They were permitted to stay at school and have all their meals at school. Parents could stay for as long as two nights and two days. Many of these parents had never been in a classroom for the deaf before they visited. When parents visited school, conferences were scheduled with the teachers, deans, principals, psychologist, audiologist, director of education, and the superintendent. Parents were urged to ask questions, see the classroom in action, and gain a total picture of what takes place in the life of their child. Many, many parents left school with a much better feeling and understanding than when they came.

A program such as this is difficult to administer and requires much time on the part of school personnel. However, the administration feels that the results are well worth the time and money spent to get the parents to the school. Even though parents are only allowed to take advantage of all these facilities once a year, exceptions are made in certain instances and parents may be invited more than once. This program has helped to bring parents closer to their children and their school.

It has given parents an opportunity to see the educational problems involved in teaching the deaf. Parents have been given the opportunity to see different teaching methods in action and they have also had the opportunity to see how their child responds in relation to his classmates. This ONE program has helped answer many of the questions which are usually raised.

Another program was writing individual letters to all parents whose children are not doing graded work, or were not following the regular curriculum of the school. For too many years in too many schools students are allowed to "drift." That is, they are promoted socially, rather than academically, until school authorities feel that the student has had enough. Then they are suddenly cut off from school. Parents naturally come roaring back with the statement that they did not know what was going on and why were they not told? This new approach is more straight forward. Parents are shown examples of regular school work, such as papers, and exams, and are able to see just what their child can or cannot do. This openness is accompanied by constructive recommendations concerning the best method of utilizing whatever potential the child may have.

In schools as large as Iowa, many students are affected and although some parents have a difficult time accepting their child's limitations, most of them are appreciative of early information, so that they can at least prepare themselves. Report cards which go out to these parents alway carry the notation "Your child is not able to do graded work and is graded only according to his own ability."

Report cards for very slow students have been abolished. Instead of the report card, letters are sent to the parent each month. In these letters a complete report is given in regard to the child's school life, dormitory life and other phases of development. Eliminating report cards has also eliminated much misunderstanding with parents.

At the present time there seems to be an increasing number of multiple handicapped students in school. Parents are concerned about what is to be done with them. If the handicap, other than deafness, is minor, then the student goes along in the regular classes for the deaf. If the handicap is serious, special classes must be provided. At Iowa special classes for these students are scheduled in all areas. Here again, the problem is a big one, but experience has shown that some of these children can and do learn. The challenge is to give them an opportunity.

At the Iowa School parents are contacted any time a child is kept in the infirmary overnight.

Parents of day pupils are encouraged to visit frequently. Because these parents live close to the school, they have ample opportunity to visit the classes.

Parents are invited to attend important school functions, such as holiday plays, homecoming activities, field day, and commencement services.

Finally, Spring Open House is a special attraction. The Friday before closing for spring vacation is parents' visitation day. All parents are encouraged to visit school. Luncheon is served to all visiting parents and they and the faculty eat together. It helps teachers and parents to enjoy a visit over a good meal. This, incidentally, is a very popular day.

The problem of parent counseling is a big one. In this complex world today it seems to be getting bigger. Much more remains to be done throughout the profession.

Parents of deaf children are entitled to know the truth about deafness and the problems which deafness creates. They are entitled to know what is being done and what can be done.

TEACHERS

It was once stated that "a teacher effects eternity: she can never tell where her influence stops."

Next to parents, teachers probably exert a greater influence on children than anyone else. In school, a teacher can make a person what he will be or a teacher can destroy potentially promising material. The tale will be told by the manner in which a teacher handles and guides children.

To be able to do an effective job of teaching, and to do all that society demands, it is important that a teacher continue to grow mentally and academically. A teacher must constantly be on his toes and examine himself critically at regular intervals to make sure that he is doing the job which he has been hired to do.

Today, education is in a precarious position. All at once Sputnik threw the world into the space age. Since that day, much criticism has been leveled at teachers. Teachers, so the critics say, are not doing an adequate job. Much public opinion accuses teachers of enjoying short working hours, long vacations, many holidays and other benefits which many teachers are receiving. In its accusations, the public singles out certain teachers who are enjoying the many benefits which education gives, but are doing nothing to deserve them. Many of these people have done nothing to help themselves professionally since the day they started to teach. These people are in very deep ruts, although many of them do not know it.

It is important that the public and the teacher understand that teaching is hard and important work. The hard-working, well prepared, enthusiastic teacher probably puts in more actual working hours in nine months than the average worker does in twelve months. In addition to the unusually heavy work load, this teacher will find time to travel, go to school, attend conventions, and do other things to grow professionally.

Things in the space age are happening so fast that only the teacher who is keeping up with the latest trends will be able to do an effective job in the classroom.

Marvin Rapp in an article entitled, "The Future Depends On You," points out that knowledge is not possible without learning, and learning is not possible without complete dedication to creativity and the disciplines of its expressions. The teacher of today must be well-trained, clear thinking, and creative. Other responsibilities of the teacher include:

1. Developing his mind
2. Exercising memory
3. Reading avidly
4. Appreciating the fine arts
5. Continuing formal schooling
6. Traveling
7. Participating in civic activities
8. Representing his school well
9. Caring for all children and establishing a good rapport with them
10. Having faith in God.

Teaching is one of the most important professions which a person can enter. It probably contributes more to the progress of civilization than any other profession. People in this profession should be proud of their status and should be ready and willing to show the public that they are doing their jobs. It is important, therefore, that they continue to grow and live for everything for which the teaching profession stands.

People in the field of education must understand that there is no room in this profession for one who is just looking for a soft job, good pay, long vacations, and other benefits which accrue to most teachers. There is no room in the teaching profession for the person who has fallen into a rut and has ceased to think and live creatively. This type of person in the teaching profession tends to destroy all for which teaching stands. It is best that this type of person leave the profession, rather than giving it a black eye.

The life of the world depends upon its teachers. Civilization can either progress or deteriorate, depending upon its educators.

It is important, therefore, that teachers realize how valuable they really are. Understanding this should impress upon teachers the importance of continuing to grow professionally.

ıust do it to be rightfully entitled to the title of

_r as school reopens, teachers return brimming with
_usıasm and ready to tackle the new year with vim and
vigor. As the year progresses, however, much of this enthusiasm
dissipates, and teaching becomes a chore.

Teaching at best is a very difficult and trying experience.
Teaching the deaf is that much more difficult. Unless a teacher
is constantly on the alert it is easy to become discouraged. This
is what enthusiasm helps to eliminate.

Experience has shown that enthusiasm rubs off. A teacher
full of enthusiasm will generate it to his students as well as to
others around him. This not only leads to better teaching, but to
happiness and satisfaction for a job well done.

Some tips from Charles Simmons may help maintain enthusiasm throughout the school year.

1. Make up your mind that you are going to be an enthusiastic
   person and don't let anything or anyone sideline you. Once
   you make up your mind to this fact, you will see that it works.
2. Don't hold back. Get up in the morning full of vim and vitality
   and let the world know about it.
3. Hear your own voice. Learn to listen to it. Most people can
   tell by the sound of your voice what kind of a mood you are in.
   Make it pleasant and you will find yourself being pleasant.
4. Associate with enthusiastic people. Enthusiastic people are lively, happy, and glad to be alive. They can also affect you psy-
   chologically. One can't afford to be around people who aren't
   cheerful and enthusiastic.
5. Make definite plans. Know what you want and how you are
   going to get it. This not only helps build enthusiasm, but helps
   put more purpose in life and gives life a design.
6. Add variety to your life. Get away from your work occasionally,
   and develop hobbies. Scientific tests show one has to have variety
   to be effective in his own work.
7. Be well groomed. Clean, neat fitting clothes as well as good personal care, helps one become confident and enthusiastic.
   Teachers set an example for students to follow. There is no
   excuse for not being well groomed at all times. Remember that
   95 per cent of what other people see are your clothes. This helps
   make an impression.
8. Take pride in your students and your school.

Remember that the school has all kinds of students, and that they all need help. A teacher can do better work by being enthusiastic with what he has, instead of complaining. He will also find that teaching will be easier and that he will be happier if he will make the most of what he has.

Try to think of your school as the best school in the nation, and that you will do your part to keep it that way.

Remember that when you criticize your own school you are in a way criticizing yourself. It does no one any good.

Finally, we must all have faith in God. As we work with these deaf children, we need the spiritual guidance that faith in God gives. Working with these children makes you a special person. You need something extra to get the job done. Faith in God will help you get it.

Remember that in the long run, enthusiasm will pay off—both for the teacher and for the student.

Chapter VIII

CONCLUSIONS

DEAF EDUCATION—AN EDUCATIONAL MIRACLE

THE GOAL OF DEAF education today is to train the hearing impaired child to take his proper place in society. It is the same goal whether the child is being taught orally, manually, simultaneously or any other method. The goal is the same whether they attend private, public, or residential schools. Even though the paths may differ, the end product is similar. The final product, the deaf adult, is an outstanding success in society not because of his handicap, but in spite of it. Employed in over 350 different occupations, the hearing impaired adult is a job holder, probably a homeowner, and a tax paying citizen. The hearing impaired adult repays his full debt to the society which made education available to him.

Knowing the successes of hearing impaired adults, it is difficult to accept some of the criticisms expressed against the school programs which produce these adults. One area of serious criticism concerns grade achievement level.

What is an achievement score? Simply stated, it is a score on any type of an achievement type instrument. There are dozens of these instruments available today and one can come up with as many scores as there are tests. For this reason, when one discusses an achievement score, it is very important to know what type of instrument is being discussed.

An achievement test score on a given achievement test indicates a score the deaf child made in comparison with thousands of *hearing children* at a given age level and at a given grade level. *This test score is not actually measuring what the child has been taught. In most instances the deaf child is being tested on material which has not been taught to him.* As an example, let us look at the reading achievement score of the deaf child since this is the score which draws the most criticism.

166

One can predict with certainty that when compared to a hearing child this score will be low by the time the deaf child finishes school. One can also predict that this achievement score is fairly close to normal during the first three years of school. Why is this? Scrutinization of the tests show that the achievement test measures what is actually being taught to the child during the first three years. After that, however, the reading program expands at such a rapid rate that the deaf child is unable to completely cope with it. As far as can be determined, methodology has nothing to do with the reading score. Deaf children could be taught by any method and the score would still remain low. With everything else being equal, it is the *ears* and the *hearing* that one has that are the key to reading achievement. The remarkable thing to remember at this point is that the deaf child *does* learn to read. It is a true miracle in that in most instances, learning to read without hearing goes against the laws of learning. The reading program for the deaf should be praised for its success rather than criticized for its limitations. Reading requires of a deaf person a degree of courage and fortitude which is not required of hearing students.

Let us look at another example. Arithmetic computation will be near the test averages. The reason for this is that mathematics comes in a neat package, and the deaf child is able to absorb it without too much difficulty. This points out to us that when we test what we have taught the deaf child, the child does well.

In summary, an achievement test score does *not* measure what the deaf child has been taught. It merely compares him to the hearing children of approximately the same age and the same grade level.

An achievement test is a dangerous instrument unless it can be understood. Many critics of deaf education do not fully understand the total picture of achievement tests and are led to untrue conclusions, which are detrimental to the deaf and to our schools.

New media and modern technology will probably raise our achievement level somewhat, but it is doubtful that we will ever be able to compare the achievement level of the deaf child with the achievement level of the hearing child until all things are equal. This means that the ears of the deaf must be unstopped. Only then can we make achievement test comparisons of the hearing and of the deaf.

Every effort must be made to conduct hard-hitting research into the causes of deafness and probable cures.

Every hearing impaired person in the United States should immediately will his ears to an ear bank. The answer to deafness may rest in the study of ears.

At times many of us in the profession of deaf education become discouraged and frustrated at our achievements and feel that we should be in a better position than we are. While it is a good thing to strive for better and more education for the hearing impaired child, it is also good to look at what has been accomplished and see how truly remarkable our schools really are.

Today, local, state, and federal governments are going all out to help the deaf. Many private organizations are also deeply involved. The adult deaf are working hand in hand to help improve themselves. This is a true tribute to the schools which have educated the hearing impaired. It is time that we saluted and complimented our schools. Schools for the deaf in the United States are doing an outstanding and remarkable job worthy of high praise.

Who are the deaf? They are *not a group*, but rather *individuals* with individual needs, individual problems, and individual approaches to living. They are made up of the same physical components of which every other human being is made. The hearing losses vary from person to person. The onset of a hearing problem is also individually unique. The personality factors and mental and physical abilities are all different for each person. Certainly people with such characteristics as these are not all the same or deserve all the same treatment. It seems an injustice to label a group under one title when no two are alike. The individualities of each human being must be recognized for what they are.

Education for everyone has a long way to go before it meets the individual needs of students. There has been failure to recognize individuality in all of education. There have been innovative developments of machines and techniques, but basically the goal is for everyone to cover the same materials and learn the same things.

"Individualizing" as it is now practiced involves the use of materials that allow a student to progress alone at his own rate of speed toward a preconceived goal that everyone must achieve. This is not individualized instruction. Truly individualized instruction would necessitate ascertaining the learning patterns of each student and then teaching to fit the students' ways of learning. Perhaps such a plan would require a different approach for each individual. Obviously, this is no easy task, but it is an essential one if the potential of each individual is to be realized. Being educated does not necessitate everyone knowing the same things. After the basic tools of learning are mastered to a sufficient degree the student should have a choice of materials to learn that lead to true knowledge and an inquisitive mind.

Schools for the deaf must accept the preceding philosophy to enable students in any hearing impaired program to meet life successfully. Schools must be willing to evaluate and revise their procedures continually without forgone conclusions or past prejudices. Such eruptive subjects as methodology should not be sidestepped any longer if the students with hearing problems are to be successfully taught as individuals. It is not being objective to force a particular method on a student without consideration of the innate learning patterns of the individual student.

Consider methodology as an example. No one method is totally satisfactory as a medium of communication. All of the approaches used today have strong and weak points. All methods can produce successful individuals and each method can expose failures.

Finger spelling requires a knowledge of spelling as words are placed in acceptable language patterns. However, spelling out words is a tedious procedure to follow endlessly.

Speechreading requires a knowledge of subject matter in order to comprehend what another is saying through visual clues.

For some individuals grasping thoughts is a natural process. For others no amount of practice seems to make speechreading a satisfactory medium of communication.

Sign language appears to be a more natural form of expression for the non-hearing as communication seems to flow with ease among those who know the language of signs. However, complete language forms are often nonexistent and the sign language, which has a limited vocabulary degenerates into less specific generalizations in time.

For those hearing impaired who can use speech intelligibly, speech is a useful means of communication. The degree of hearing and the onset of deafness are two factors that relate closely in speech. Usually profound deafness from an early age prohibits a person from accomplishing speech which is intelligible to anyone beyond a close circle of family and friends.

The only sensible conclusion that can be reached concerning methodology seems to be that the method of communication be suited to each individual child. The child or student must be the center of attention. Then, and only then, can the best solution to that individual's needs be met. This same approach should not be limited to methodology but it should be the focal point for all thinking concerning an individual's welfare in and out of school. The need for true individualization cannot be overemphasized.

Another point that deserves consideration in establishing an appropriate goal for any person with hearing impairment is the need to educate so that deafness is not an excuse for not succeeding or meeting life satisfactorily. If a person is educated as an individual, the maturation of a student should develop personal responsibility for self. With a good background in school, a person should be ready to accept responsibility and establish personal goals without the need of using an escape crutch for failure to do what is wanted. Deafness obviously can make adjustments to living necessary, but it is not an insurmountable obstacle in achieving a satisfying life in any strata of living a person may desire.

Deaf education is a continually progressing profession. The types of deafness continue to be varied and the complexities of the multiply handicapped add to the challenge. New ideas and techniques are being expressed and explored daily. New equipment and new concepts of the physical aspects of schools are regularly announced. The expectations for students with impaired hearing have never been higher. Goals of excellence in education are realistic. The students themselves expect the best and establish goals of high calibre. Their dreams cannot be questioned and should not be denied. Adults of unsurpassed quality living in today's world is an achieveable goal. A variety of educational methods have been employed to successfully accomplish the many facets of deaf education, but the goal to reach the mountaintop should be striven for with enthusiasm and zeal in a positive approach through individualistic education for all of the hearing impaired.

BIBLIOGRAPHY

1. ARTLEY, A. S.: *Criteria for Selecting Materials and Instruments for Corrective Reading.* Chicago, U. of Chicago, 1953.
2. ARTLEY, A. S.: *Criteria for Selecting Materials for Reading.* Chicago, U. of Chicago, 1953.
3. BARNETTE, GASPER: *Tachistoscopic Teaching Techniques.* Dubuque, Iowa, Brown, W. C., 1955.
4. BENDER, RUTH: *The Conquest of Deafness.* Cleveland, Western Reserve, 1960.
5. BIRCH, JACK W.: *Retrieving the Retarded Reader.* Bloomington, Ill., Public School Pub., 1955.
6. BIRCH, J., and BIRCH, JANE: The Leiter International Performance Scale as an aid in the psychological study of deaf children. *Amer Ann Deaf, 96*:502-511, 1951.
7. BIRCH, J., and BIRCH, JANE: Predicting school achievement in young deaf children. *Amer Ann Deaf, 101*:348-352, 1956.
8. BISHOP, H. M.: Performance scale tests applied to deaf and hard-of-hearing children. *Volta Rev, 38*:447-463, 1936.
9. BLOOM, B. S., and KRATHWOHL, D. R.: *Taxonomy of Educational Objectives: Handbook I.* London, Longman's, 1956.
10. BOATNER, MAXINE T.: *Voice of the Deaf.* Washington, Pub. Affairs, 1959.
11. BRIDGEMAN, O.: The estimation of mental abilities in deaf children. *Amer Ann Deaf, 84*:337-349, 1939.
12. BRUNER, JEROME S.: *On Knowing, Essays for the Left Hand.* Cambridge Mass., Belknap Press of Harvard, 1964.
13. BRUNER, JEROME S.: *The Process of Education.* Cambridge, Mass., Harvard, 1962.
14. CORRY, P. B.: Deaf children see and learn. *Education Screen,* April, 1953.
15. DARRELL and SULLIVAN: *Building Word Power,* New York, World Book, 1941.
16. DEBARDNIS, A.: Audio-visual reading tools. *Grade Teacher,* April, 1955, p. 33.
17. DELAND, F.: *The Story of Lip Reading.* Washington, Volta Bureau, 1931.
18. FARRAR, A. (Ed.): *Arnold on the Education of the Deaf.* London, Francis Carter, 1923.
19. FENTON, EDWIN: *The New Social Studies in Secondary Schools.* New York, Holt, 1966.

20. GARNETT, C. B., JR.: *The Exchange of Letters Between Samuel Heinicke and Abbꞓ Charles Michel De L'Epee.* New York, Vantage, 1968.

21. GIANGRECO, C. J.: *The Hiskey-Nebraska Test of Learning Aptitude as a Predictor of Academic Achievement of Deaf Children.* Lincoln, U. of Neb., 1965.

22. GRAY, WM.: *On Their Own in Reading.* Chicago, Scott, 1956.

23. GREENBERGER, D.: Doubtful cases. *Amer Ann Deaf, 34:*93, 1889.

24. HARDY, W. G.: Children with impaired hearing; an audiologic perspective. *Children's Bureau Pub. No. 326.*

25. HILGARD, E. R.: *Theories of Learning.* New York, Appleton, 1956.

26. HILL, MINER C. (as told to Adele Whitely Fletcher): "The greatest thing you can give your child." *Family Weekly,* April 28, 1963.

27. HISKEY, M. S.: Manual, Neb. Test of Learning Aptitude, Lincoln, U. of Neb., 1941.

28. HISKEY, M. S.: Norms for children with hearing for the Nebraska Test of Hearing Aptitude. *J Educ Research, 51:*137-143, 1957.

29. HODGSON, K.: The Deaf and their Problems. New York, Philosophical, Lib., 1953.

30. HUCK, C.: Many methods and materials. *Childhood Education,* October, 1963.

31. ITARD, J. M.; *The Wild Boy of Aveyron.* New York, Appleton, 1962.

32. KLINE, T. K.: A study of free association tests with deaf children. *Amer Ann Deaf, 90:*237-258, 1945.

33. LANE, HELEN S., and MACPHERSON, J. G.: A comparison of deaf and hearing on the Hiskey test and on performance scales. *Amer Ann Deaf, 93:*178-184, 1948.

34. LARR, A. L., and CAIN, E. R.: Measurement of native ability of deaf children. *Volta Rev, 61:*160-163, 1959.

35. LEVINE, EDNA S.: *The Psychology of Deafness.* New York, Columbia, 1960.

36. LEVINE, EDNA S.: Studies in psychological evaluation of the deaf. *Volta Rev, 65:*496-512, 1963.

37. LEVINE, EDNA S.: *Youth in a Soundless World.* New York, New York University Press, 1956.

38. LOVE, J. K.: *The Deaf Child.* New York, Wm. Wood, 1911.

39. LOVE, J. K., and ADDISON, W. H.: *Deaf Mutism.* Glasgow, James MacLehose and Sons, 1896.

40. MACKANE, K.: A comparison of intelligence of deaf and hearing children. *Teachers' College Contributions to Education, No. 585.* New York, Columbia, 1933.

41. MACMILLAN, D. P., and BRUNER, F. G.: Children attending the public day schools for the deaf in Chicago. *Special Report of the Department of Child Study and Pedagogic Investigation.* Chicago, Chicago Public Schools, 1906.

42. MEEK, H. S.: Breaking the barrier of deafness. *Times Educational Supplement,* January 21, 1955, p. 21.
43. MOTT, A. J.: The ninth year of a deaf child's life. *Amer Ann Deaf, 44:* 401-412, 1899.
44. MYKLEBUST, H.: *Psychology of Deafness.* New York, Grune, 1960.
45. MYKLEBUST, H.: *Toward a New Understanding of the Deaf Child.* Proceedings of the Thirty-sixth Meeting of the Convention of American Instructors of the Deaf. Document No. 103. Washington, U. S. Government Printing Office, 1953.
46. MYKLEBUST, HELMER: *Towards a Better Understanding of the Deaf Child.* Procedings of the Conference of Executives of American Schools for the Deaf, 1960.
47. NEWLEE, C. E.: A report of learning tests with deaf children. *Volta Rev, 21:*216-223, 1919.
48. OSTERN, B.: Use of a movie film in a class of the deaf. *Volta Rev,* May, 1953.
49. PINTNER, R., and PATTERSON, O. G.: The Binet Scale and the deaf child. *J Ed Psychol., 6:*201-210, 1915.
50. PINTNER, R., and PATTERSON, O. G.: Learning tests with deaf children. Psychol. Monogr, 20:196-198, 1916.
51. ROBINSON, HELEN: *Corrective Reading in Classroom and Clinic.* Chicago, U. of Chicago, 1953.
52. RUSSEL, W. F.: *How to Teach Silent Reading to Beginners.* New York, Lippincott, 1930.
53. SCHICK, HELEN F.: A Performance test for deaf children of school age. *Volta Rev, 36:*651-658, 1934.
54. SMITH: *One Hundred Ways to Teach Silent Reading.* New York, World Book, 1935.
55. STUNKEL, EVA R.: The performance of deaf and hearing college students on verbal and non-verbal intelligence test. *Amer Ann Deaf, 102:*342-355, 1957.
56. TAYLOR, H.: A spelling test. *Amer Ann Deaf, 43:*41-45, 1898.
57. TEMPLIN, MILDREN C.: Review of the Nebraska Test of Learning Aptitude. In Buros, O. K. (Ed.): *The Fourth Mental Measurements.* Highland Park, New Jersey, Cryphon, 1951, p. 484.
58. THOMPSON, H. M.: *A Plan for Better Reading.* New York, Holt, 1956.
59. WAITE, HELEN E.: *Make a Joyful Sound.* Philadelphia, Macrae Smith, 1961.
60. Working together to improve a reading program. *National Elementary Principal,* September, 1955, p. 47.
61. ZEKEL, A., and VAN DER KALK, J. J.: A comparative intelligence test of groups of children born deaf and of good hearing by means of the Porteus Test. *Amer Ann Deaf, 84:*114-123, 1939.

INDEX

A

Abstract, teaching the, 82
Achievement score, 166-7
Activities, extra curricular, 107-14
  preschool, 32
Administrator, 150-61
Adult deaf, 25, 115-21
Age, mental *vs.* learning, 142
Agricola, 6, 11
Alexander Graham Bell Association
  for the Deaf, 26, 45
Alexander, W. G., 47
Alphabet, 8
  manual, 132, 169
  one-handed Spanish, 13
American Annals of the Deaf, 92
American Association to Promote the
  Teaching of Speech to the
  Deaf, 26
American Asylum for the Deaf and
  Dumb, 23-4
American Hearing Society, 45
American Instructors of the Deaf,
  Convention of, 45, 150
  Proceedings, 92
American Laryngology, Rhinology and
  Otology Society, 128-9
American Medical Association, 45
American Speech and Hearing Asso-
  ciation, 45
Amman, J. K., 11
Amplification, 29, 42-3, 57
Anxiety, 38
Arithmetic, 52, 146, 151, 167
Arthur Point Scale Performance Test,
  135-7
Asylum, 20
  American, for the Deaf and Dumb,
  24
  see also School
Athletics, 110-1, 113, 127
Audio-visual aid, 82-3, 86
Audiogram, 42

Audiologist, 42
Audiometer, 42
Augustine, St., 5
Aristotle, vii, 3, 5

B

Baker, H., 13
Bebain, R. A. A., 16
Bedtime, 125
Beethoven, L. von, 20
Belgium, 10
Bell, A. G., 25, 26-8
Bell, A. M., 25-6
Bell, Mabel Hubbard, 25, 26-7
Bell Symbols, 26
Beltone Electronics, 46
Bender, Ruth, 4-5, 6, 7, 15, 21-2, 28
Better Business Bureau, 42
Bible, vii, 4, 5
Binet Scale, Stanford revision, 136,
  138
Binet-Simon Scale for Measurement
  Intelligence, 132-3
Birch, J. and J., 137, 138
Bishop, H. M., 135-6
Blackboard, 64-5
Blind-deaf, 25
Boatner, Maxine, 24, 28
Bolling family, 22
Bonet, J. P., 7-8, 9
Book, 39, 47, 58, 84
Boston, 25
Boston School for Deaf Mutes, 25, 26
Braidwood, T., 17, 18, 23
Bridgeman, O., 136
Bruner, F. G., 131-2
Bruner, J., 99
Bulwer, J., 9

C

Cain, E. R., 138
Campbell Soup Co., 119

177

Campus life, 93-4
Canada, 47
Canal, semicircular, 19
Candidate, political, 94
Cape Kennedy Space Program, 119
Cardano, G., 6, 7, 11, 15
Carrier, hearing aid, 43
Casaubon, M., 10
Central Institute, St. Louis, 135
Century, sixteenth, vii, 6-7
  seventeenth, vii, 7-11
  eighteenth, 11-19
  nineteenth, 19-29
  twentieth, 29-30
Character, ethical, 53, 153
Chores and privileges, 125
Christianity, 5
Citizenship, 52-3, 152
City mission, 21
Clarke, J., 25
Clarke School for the Deaf, 25
Classroom, 84
  discussion in, 76
  news period, 63-72
Clerc, L., 16, 24
Clinic, hearing and speech, 42
  John Tracy, 46
Club, 94
Cogswell, Alice, 23
Colorado School for the Deaf, 150
Columbia Institution for the Deaf, 29
Comenius, J. A., 7, 60
Communication, verbal, 130; *see also·*
  Speech
Community, 116
Conant, J., 97
Conference of Executives of American
  Schools for the Deaf, 31, 45
Congress, 29, 120
Control, hearing aid, 44
Controlled Reader, 83
Conversation, 124
Coordination, 40
Cord, hearing aid, 43
Council Bluffs, xiii, 113
Council Bluffs Nonpareil, 116, 127
Council for Exceptional Children, 46
Counselors and counseling, 100, 104,
  156

parental, 158-61
Crime and delinquency, 53
Curriculum, 54-114, 155
Cushing, Fanny, 25

D

Dalgarno, G., 10, 15
Dating, 102, 108-9
Deaf-blind, 25
Deaf Child, The, 30
Deafness Research Foundation, 128-9
Defoe, Daniel, 10, 13
Deland, F., 11, 17
de l'Epee, C. M., 14-6, 18, 24
Denmark, 21
Development, social, 125
Difference, deaf vs. general public,
  3-7
Digby, Sir K., 8-9
Digit-Symbol Test, 133, 134
Directory, 83
Disbrow, Co., 119
Discipline, 32, 38
Dolch materials, 78, 81
Doll, E. A., 33
Dormitory, 79, 87, 107-14
Downs, M. P., 47
Drama, 12, 61
Drever-Collins Test, 135
Drug, 29
Duvall, S. and E., 106

E

Ear bank, 168; *see also* Temporal
  bone bank
Earmold, 44
Easter Seal Research Foundation, 46
Education, higher, 114
Education of Man, The, 18
Education, State Department of, 45
Election, mock, 94
Elstad, L., 29, 58
Emotional problem, reading and, 79
England, 8-10, 13, 22
English, 60-78, 155
  elementary, 61-73
  junior high and high school, 73-8
Enrichment, 61

Equipment, auditory, *see* Hearing aid, Amplification
Ewing, I. R., 47

F

Family, 102
  relationship of deaf child, 122-6
  see also Home
Farm, 87
Farrar, A., 4, 6, 18
Federal Service Entrance Examination, 139
Feedback, 44
Fenton, E., 90, 91
Film, 48, 83
Finger spelling, 169; *see also* Manual method, Alphabet
Finland, 21
Fischer Table, 144
Formalism, 22
Fowler, Sophia, 24
France, 13, 21
Free time, 110-4; *see also* Leisure, Recreation
French Academy of Science, 13
Froebel, F., 18

G

Gallaudet, E. M., 24, 28-9
Gallaudet, T. H., 16, 23-4, 25, 26, 28, 29
Gallaudet College, 29, 45, 57, 58, 63, 114, 139
Gates Reading Test, 144-6
Geography, 67-8; *see also* Social Studies
Germany, 12, 16, 20
Gesel, A., 80
Gesture, natural, 22
Giangreco, speech by, 150-8
  study by, 144-9
Glasgow, 21
God, 5, 163, 165
Goldsmith, O., 12
Goodenough Draw-A-Man Test, 134, 137
Grades and grading, 58-9, 74; *see also* Report card

Graeser, J. B., 21
Grammar, 74
Green, F., 22
Greenberger, D., 130-1
Group intelligence test, 133
Guidance, 100-3; *see also* Counselor

H

Hall, P., Sr., 29
Handicapped, multiple, 161
Hard-of-hearing *vs* deaf, 20
Harris, G. M., 47
Hartford, 24, 25, 28
Health, 52, 150-1
Healy Scale Information Test, 136
Hearing, 54-8
  experience with, people, 113
Hearing aid, 18, 29, 41-4, 57
  manufacturers, 46
Hebrew, vii
Heinicke, S., 16-7, 18, 20
Herbart, J. F., 22
Heredity, 19
Hill, F. M., 21, 22
Hill, M. C., 124
Hiskey, M. S., 140-1
Hiskey-Nebraska Test of Learning Aptitude, Revised, 90, 144, 146-7
Hiskey Test, 140-4
History, 67-8
  of deaf education, 3-30
History of the Life and Adventures of Mr. Duncan Campbell, 10
Hodgson, K., 3, 8, 11, 12, 13-4, 15, 16, 17-8, 19-20, 20-1, 22, 28
Holder, W., 9-10
Holiday, 94; *see also* Summer
Holland, 11
Home, 53, 151
  training, 38-41
  see also Family
Horace Mann School, 25
House parent, 79, 87, 110-1, 156
Hoversten, G., 47
Howe, S. G., 25
Hubbard, G., 25
Hubbard (Bell), Mabel, 25, 26

Human and Criminal Institutions of New York, 23

I

Immature child, 80
Indifference, 32
Intelligence quotient, 130-49
International Parents' Organization, 45
Iowa, xi, 87, 93
   Univ. of, 59
Iowa Board of Regents, 128
Iowa Hawkeye, 54
Iowa School for the Deaf, ix, xiii, 31, 54-5, 90, 93, 98, 103, 104, 108-14, 128, 153, 159-61
Itard, J. M. G., 19

J

Jesus, vii, 5
Job, loss of, 106
   placement in, 102
   see also Occupation
John Tracy Clinic, 46
Johnson, E., 86
Justinian Code, 4-5

K

Keaster, J., 47
Kendall, A., 28
Kendall School, 29, 63
Kline, T. K., 137
Kindergarten, 98

L

Lag, educational, 125
Language, 40-1, 61-2, 67-8
   sign, 58, 132, 170
Larr, A. L., 138-9
Law, Old Testament, 4
   Roman, 4-5
Leadership, 157
Learning, listening approach to, 57
   realism a principle, 7
   theory of, 912
Learning age, 142

Leisure, 53, 152-3; *see also* Recreation, Free time
Leiter Test, 137
Levine, E. S., 130
Library, 76, 82, 84, 87
Lincoln, A., 29
Lippitt, Jeanie, 25
Lipreading, 13, 45; *see also* Speechreading
Listening, 57
Literature, 61
Locke, J., 7
Love, J. K., 30
Love and affection, 124
Luther, M., 6

M

MacKane, K., 134-5
MacMillan, D. P., 131-2
Maico Electronics, 46
Mann, H., 24-5
Manners, 109
Manual method, 17, 18, 28
Mardi Gras, 113
Marriage, 102
Massachusetts, 22
Mastercraft, 119
Mathematics, 98-100
Maturation, 4, 80, 98, 125
McLeland, Shirley, 115
Meals, 125
Media, news, as aid to schools, 125-8
   work, 76, 82-3
Medicine, 18, 29; *see also* Operation, Research
Mendel's Laws, 19
Mental age, 142
Method, 169-70
   Amman's, 11
   Bell's, 27-8
   Braidwood's, 17
   combination, 28
   "mother," of Pestalozzi, 21
   oral *vs* manual, 17, 24, 30
Meyer, M. F., 135
Montessori, Marie, 19
Mother method, 21
Motivation theory, 92

Mott, A. J., 131
Movies, 87, 109
Music, 41
Myklebust, H. R., 3, 47, 124, 139

N

National Education Association, 51-2
National Institute for the Deaf, 114
National Society for Crippled Children and Adults, 46
Nature, 41, 63, 87
Nebraska, Univ. of, 144
Nebraska Test of Learning Aptitude for Young Deaf Children, 137-8, 139, 140-4
New Life for Jennifer, 48
New York Institution for the Deaf and Dumb, 23
Newlee, C. E., 134
News, classroom, 63-72
  media and schools, 126-8
Northampton, Mass., 25
Northwestern Univ., 124

O

Occupation, 106-7, 118-9
Old Testament, vii, 4
Omaha, 119
  Univ. of, 59
Omaha Evening World-Herald, 88
Ontario School Ability Test, 136, 138
Operation, 29
  middle ear, 19, 48
Oral method or philosophy, 16, 17, 25, 26, 28
Otologist, 42
Overproduction and overindulgence, 32

P

Pamphlet, 47
Paragraphing, 67, 77
Paralipomenom, 6
Parent, 31, 38, 58-9, 79, 86-7, 116, 158-61
  attitudes, 123-6
Paris, 19

Patterson, O. G., 132, 133, 134
Pediatrician, 32
Pendleton, 119
Pereira, J. R., 13-4
Perkins Institute for the Blind, 25
Pestalozzi, J. H., 18, 21, 93
Philosophy, 168
Picture, 39, 40
Pintner, R., 132, 133, 134
Pliny, 4
Pollack, D. C., 47
Ponce de Leon, P., 7, 11
Porter, Sylvia, 105, 106
Porteus Maze Test, 136
Post-school, 115-21
Prehistoric time, 4
Preschool, 31-47
  environment, emotional, 31-2
    physical, 33-8
  hearing aid, 41-4
  home training, 38-41
  professional help, 44-7
Principal, 150-61
Program, academic, 104
  parent visitation, 159-60
  reading, 80, 84-5
  recreation, 109-14
  school, 53, 54-5
  see also Curriculum
Progress, to report, 58-9; *see also* Report card
Psychology, 90, 91, 130-49
Public, 29; *see also* Society

Q

Quarreling, 32

R

Radio, 87
Radioear Corp., 46
Randall's Island Performance Series, 135, 136
Rapp, M., 162-3
Reader, Controlled, 83
  supplemental, 81-2
Reading, 52, 78-87, 151, 166-7
  series, 78
  social studies and, ability, 90

Recreation, 109-14
  coeducational, 109
  see also Leisure
Rejection, 32
Religious training, 125
Report card, 160-1; *see also* Grades,
    Progress
Research, medical, 128-9; *see also*
    Operation
Residual hearing, 40, 56
Responsibility, 32
Retardation, 132, 134
  reading, 79
  see also Intelligence quotient
Rickenbacker, E., 88-9
Rinne, H. A., 20
Robinson, G. C., 47
Rochester Institute of Technology,
    114
Rogers, Harriet, 25
Rousseau, J. J., 14
Royal Society, 13
Rules and regulations, 108-14
Russia, 21

S

Safety, 41
St. Paul, Minn., 135
Schick, Helen, 135
School, 29
  American public, 49-54
    basic philosophy, 50
    education principles, 51-4
    student, 51
    teacher, 50-1
  Boston, for Deaf Mutes, 25, 26
  Clarke, for the Deaf, 25
  Colorado, for the Deaf, 150
  Horace Mann, 25
  Iowa, for the Deaf, ix, xiii, 31,
    54-5, 90, 93, 98, 103, 104,
    108-14, 128, 155, 159-61
  Kendall, 29
  New York Institution for the Deaf
    and Dumb, 23
  oral, 25
  residential, viii, 79, 85, 103, 126
  state, beginning of, 12, 24

Western Pennsylvania, for the Deaf,
    137
  see also Asylum
Science, 95-8
Scotland, 10
Scouting, 113
Secrecy instructing the deaf, 12, 16,
    17
Sense training, 7
Sentence, 65, 67, 77
Sequin, E., 19
Serta, 119
Shop, vocational, 105-6
Skill, landmark, 33-8
  vocational, 52
Sicard, Abbe R. A. C., 16, 21, 24
Silent World—Muffled World, 48
Simmons, C., 164
*Simplification of the Alphabet and
    the Method of Teaching Deaf
    Mutes to Speak,* 7
Social hygiene, 102
Social studies, 88-95
  reading ability and, 90
  status of, 89
Society, adjustment to, 107, 113,
    116-20
Sonotone Corp., 46
Sound, amplified, 42
  source of, 41
Spain, 6, 7-8
Spartan viewpoint, 5
Specialist, reading, 85, 86
Speech, 11, 13, 16, 26, 45, 58-9, 61,
    65, 170
Speechreading, 11, 26, 27, 59-60, 124,
    169-70; *see also* Lipreading
Spelling, 66
  finger, 169
Spiral curriculum, 97
Spring Open House, 161
Staff, home relationships of, 53
Stanford, J., 23
Stanford Achievement Test, 90, 93,
    144
State University of Iowa, 118
Stubbornness, 32
Student, 51, 56
  junior and senior, trip, 94

potential college, 103
relationship with teacher, 59-60
teaching fellow, 59
Stunkel, E. R., 139
Summer, 87
Survey, national, 127
Switzerland, 11
Symbol-Digit Test, 133, 134

T

Tachistoscope, 83
Taylor, H., 131
Teacher, 13-8, 50-1, 78, 82, 87, 92,
    157, 162-4
relationship with student, 59-60
Teacher Rating Scale, Giangreco,
    144-6
Team, athletic, 111
total school, 93-4
Teen Topics, 127
Telephone, 26
Television, 87
Temper tantrum, 32
Templin, Mildred, 143
Temporal bone bank, 128-9; *see also*
    Ear bank
Test, aptitude, 104
Arthur Point Scale Performance,
    135, 136, 137-8
Binet-Simon, 132-3
diagnostic, 84
Digit-Symbol, 133, 134
Drever-Collins, 135
Gates Reading, 144-6
Goodenough Draw-A-Man, 134,
    137-8
Healy Scale Information, 136
Hiskey-Nebraska, of Learning Ap-
    titude Revised, 90, 144, 146-7
Leiter, 137-8
Metropolitan Achievement, 144-6
Nebraska, of Learning Aptitude,
    137-8, 139, 140-4
Ontario School Ability, 136, 138
Porteus Maze, 136
Stanford Achievement, 90, 93, 144
Symbol-Digit, 133, 134
Wechsler-Bellevue Intelligence, 139

Testing IQ, 130-49
Textbook, 74, 81, 82, 126
Theme, writing a, 74-7
subjects, 75-7
Theory, learning, 91-2
motivation, 92
resonance, 20
telephone, 20
transfer, 92
Thinking, conceptual, 82
Training, auditory, 57
home, 38-41
on-the-job, 102
preschool, 31
religious, 125
vocational, 103-6
Trip, field, 76, 83, 86, 94, 113
junior and senior, 94, 113
True, Mary, 25
Tuning fork, 20

U

Unemployment, 105, 106
United Nations, 89
United States, 14, 16, 22, 23, 47,
    88, 89
Utley, J., 47

V

van der Kolk, J. J., 136-7
Van Wyk, M. K., 47
Velasco family, 6
Don Luis de, 8-9
Verb, 65
Vicon Instrument Co., 46
Victor, Wild Boy of Aveyron, 19
Vindication of the Rights of Women,
    12
Vineland Social Maturity Scale, 33-8
Virginia, 22-3
Visual aid, 82
Vocabulary, 65, 67, 76, 78, 80-1,
    117-8
Vocational efficiency, 52, 151-2
Vocational Rehabilitation, 120
State Department of, 103
Vocational training, 103-6
Voice of the Deaf, 28

Volta Bureau, 26, 45, 47
Volta Review, The, 45, 92
von Helmholtz, H., 20
von Helmont, F. M., Baron, 10

W

Wallis, J., 9-10, 13
Washington, 28
Washington Conference, 28
Watson, J., 20
Wax, 44
Weather report, 64, 72
Wechsler-Bellevue Intelligence Test, 139
Wechsler Intelligence Scale for Children, 138-9

Wechsler's Adult Intelligence Scale, Form I, 37
Western Pennsylvania School for the Deaf, 137
White Sands, N. M., 119
Wild Boy of Aveyron, 19
Wollstonecraft, Mary, 12
Word list, 68-73
  Dolch, 78, 81
Work, *see* Occupation
Worker, skilled and unskilled, 105
Writing, 52, 151; *see also* English

X, Y, Z

Y-Teens, 113
Zekel, A., 136-7
Zenith Corp., 46